THE REVOLUTIONARY LIFE OF FREDA BEDI

(Courtesy John Hills)

THE REVOLUTIONARY LIFE OF

Freda Bedi

BRITISH FEMINIST, INDIAN NATIONALIST, BUDDHIST NUN

Vicki Mackenzie

Foreword by Jetsunma Tenzin Palmo

SHAMBHALA · BOULDER · 2017

Shambhala Publications, Inc.
4720 Walnut Street
Boulder, CO 80301
www.shambhala.com

9 8 7 6 5 4 3 2 1

FIRST EDITION
Printed in the United States of America

♾ This edition is printed on acid-free paper that meets
the American National Standards Institute z39.48 Standard.
♻ This book is printed on 30% postconsumer recycled paper.
For more information please visit www.shambhala.com.
Distributed in the United States by Penguin Random House LLC
and in Canada by Random House of Canada Ltd

Designed by Lance Hidy

LIBRARY OF CONGRESS CATALOGING-IN-PUBLICATION DATA
Names: Mackenzie, Vicki, author.
Title: The revolutionary life of Freda Bedi: British Feminist, Indian Nationalist, Buddhist Nun / Vicki MacKenzie.
Description: First edition. | Boulder, CO: Shambhala, 2017.
Identifiers: LCCN 2016028308 | ISBN 9781611804256 (paperback)
Subjects: LCSH: Bedi, Freda, 1911–1977. | Buddhist women—Biography. |
Buddhist nuns—Biography. | BISAC:RELIGION / Buddhism /
Tibetan. | BIOGRAPHY & AUTOBIOGRAPHY / Religious. |
BIOGRAPHY & AUTOBIOGRAPHY / Women.
Classification: LCC BQ942.E38 M33 2017 | DDC 294.3/923092 [B]—
dc 3 LC record available at https://lccn.loc.gov/2016028308

To all mothers everywhere, especially my own inexpressibly kind mother, Irene Mackenzie (1919–1998), in gratitude for her unfailing love and support.

CONTENTS

FOREWORD

H ERE AT LAST is the long-awaited biography of a remarkable
woman named Freda Bedi or Sister Khechog Palmo, who was
a pioneering figure in the early years of the Tibetan exile in India.
A wife, mother, and former freedom fighter in the Indian Independence movement, Freda went on to become one of the first Western nuns in Tibetan Buddhism and was the founder of a school for
young reincarnate lamas and also the founder of the first Tibetan
nunnery in India. She was a close disciple of the Sixteenth Karmapa—instrumental in his first visit to the United States—and was
also the mentor of Chögyam Trungpa Rinpoche, along with many
other lamas who brought Tibetan Buddhism to the West.

Her outreach and enlightened projects empowered so many
others during the early days of the Tibetan exile and deserve to
be remembered and appreciated. So I am indeed grateful to Vicki
Mackenzie for her efforts to recover so much biographical material,
before it is too late, in order to tell us the inspiring story of Sister
Palmo's extraordinary life and her contribution to the preservation
of the Tibetan dharma during a time of precarious transition.

—Jetsunma Tenzin Palmo

INTRODUCTION: FIRST GLIMPSE

I MISSED HER by a few short weeks, which in the light of what
was to transpire many years later was a great pity. By the time
I trekked up the washed-away dirt road to that magical hilltop
monastery called Kopan, peering over the Kathmandu Valley, for
my first-ever meditation course on a bright November morning in
1976, everyone was still talking about it. One afternoon, the senior
lama—a round, charismatic character named Thubten Yeshe—had
walked into the meditation tent, ushering before him a tall, beautiful, somewhat stout Western woman in her mid-sixties. She had
fair skin, blue eyes, a perfectly round face, and a decidedly dignified
bearing. She had the bald head of a Buddhist nun and was wearing
maroon and yellow robes. Much to the onlookers' bemusement,
Lama Yeshe proceeded to lead her to the high brocaded throne, and
when she was settled, stood before her, brought his hands together
at his heart, and reverently threw himself on the floor in three full-
length body prostrations.

The course participants, who had never seen (or indeed heard of)
any female on a throne, let alone a Westerner in fancy robes, were
taken aback. In this patriarchal religion, living women were never
bowed to. But if Lama Yeshe held this woman in high regard, she
had to be special, because over the weeks they had come to respect
this kind, powerful man who had spoken out of his own wisdom
and made them laugh.

The woman's name was Freda Bedi, born in Derby, in England's
Midlands region, the daughter of a watchmaker, who had married
a Sikh whose last name was Bedi.

I thought no more about it—then. Back in 1976, I was far more

excited by the prospect of sampling the very radical business of meditation, delivered by "exotic" and mysterious lamas only recently
emerged from their secret, forbidden land of Tibet. Here was high
adventure. I had crept away from my job as a feature writer on one
of Britain's leading national newspapers in the heart of London's
Fleet Street without telling anyone what I was doing. In those days
Buddhism was so unknown in the West, it was regarded virtually
as a cult—foreign, full of heretical beliefs, and highly dangerous. I
knew I would have lost all credibility as a responsible, serious journalist if I had revealed where I was going.

I was drawn there not just by curiosity to tread the unknown
path (an essential quality for a journalist) but by some nonspecific,
sincerely felt need to explore the deeper meaning of things that
lay beyond the "getting and spending," as Wordsworth put it. This
quiet yearning had been with me since childhood, and over the
years as my Christian background failed to deliver what I sought, I
began to feel drawn to the East, intuitively suspecting their ancient
wisdom might hold what I was looking for.

Kopan and the lamas didn't disappoint. What I discovered on my
clandestine journey was fascinating and fulfilling enough to keep
me engrossed for forty years. During that time Freda Bedi's name
continued to crop up, dropped into the conversation by people who
had met her in the very early days of Tibetan Buddhism's appearance in the outside world. Everyone spoke of her with affection and
a little awe. I heard that she had had a stellar career, was a household
name in India, as well as being the mother of three children—one
of whom was a handsome Bollywood star and a James Bond villain.

Something radical had happened to Freda Bedi in her middle
age, because she turned her back on her fame, her work, and her
family and had become the first Western Tibetan Buddhist nun. I
learned that she had started a school for the young reincarnated
lamas when they were refugees newly arrived in India, to teach
them English and the ways of the world. One of her pupils was
Zopa Rinpoche, Lama Yeshe's heart disciple, who had taught me
first in Kopan and subsequently in other venues around the world.
Freda had plucked him out of a terrible disease-ridden refugee

camp, a skinny kid wracked with tuberculosis, provided him with medicines, new robes, a sponsor, and the beginnings of a Western education.

Maybe that was why Lama Yeshe, always full of gratitude, had bowed before her.

Other tidbits about Freda came my way. Strangely, this subtle amassing of information gathered momentum as time went by, as though something I was not conscious of was building up. I discovered that she had been a freedom fighter for the cause of Indian independence, joining Gandhi's powerful movement in defiance of her own people, the British. And she had gone to jail for her trouble, the first Englishwoman to do so. My journalist's antennae began to twitch. Maybe there was a story here. Freda was becoming increasingly interesting.

As my experience with the Tibetan Buddhist world grew, I heard something about Freda that surprised me. Among the Tibetans it was whispered that Freda was regarded as an emanation of Tara, the female Buddha of Compassion in Action. Tara, (beloved of all Tibetans, religious or not) was hailed as the Divine Mother, to whom they all prayed when in need. It was Tara, rather than the historical male Shakyamuni Buddha, whom they called upon whenever they were in danger, sad, frightened, or sick, because they knew Tara did not merely sit and listen compassionately to their pleas; she got up and *did* something. This ability to act and act quickly was regarded as a quintessential female quality.

Over the years I had seen plenty of paintings and statues of Tara. She certainly looked nothing like a fair-skinned, blue-eyed English-woman. Usually she was painted green (although sometimes white and other colors), with a round, moon-shaped face, a benign expression, and one leg stretched out ready to spring into action. Could Freda Bedi possibly be a divine being? It seemed ludicrous—heretical even. Why and how had she earned this accolade? Freda, apparently, had appeared in the darkest time of Tibet's history, when the Dalai Lama and thousands of his fellow countrymen, women, and children had fled over the Himalayas in a terrifying trek to freedom. They had poured into exile, sick and traumatized by the persecution and torture they had experienced and by their highly dangerous escape. Freda has been there to comfort them, bathe their wounds, soothe their fears, and help put them back on their feet.

As one, they began to call her "Mummy"—and then "Mummy-la," the suffix denoting an honorific attributed to anyone held in high esteem. Freda had become so identified with this title that even Westerners began to call her that.

Curiously, at the beginning of the new millennium I was approached by various people asking that I write a book about Freda Bedi. One of the most insistent was the English nun Tenzin Palmo, who had met Freda when she was just twenty years old before disappearing into a Himalayan cave for twelve years to meditate, and then emerging as a brilliant, globally recognized teacher. I had recently finished writing Tenzin Palmo's biography, *Cave in the Snow*. "Freda is an inspirational woman, a role model for women everywhere. We need real-life examples of powerful women, especially nuns. Besides, Freda's life was enormous. She was a pioneer in so many fields," she had said.

Then Freda's children approached me, asking me to chronicle their mother's life. I was honored, but demurred. My strongest resource, Freda herself, was not around. Sadly, she had died just a few months after she had appeared in Kopan in 1976. She was sixty-six years old. And I had missed her. Had I known then that I would write her book, I would have sought her out, requesting access to her time, memories, and detailed accounts of her life. As a journalist that was my preferred way of working. How else could I accurately assess her character, her motives, the minutiae of her daily life, her conflicts—the necessary components for creating a vivid, accurate portrait of a human being?

It was when I heard that the Dalai Lama himself was asking why a book on her had never been written that I capitulated. If the Dalai Lama thought Freda Bedi's life was worth recording, who was I to argue? I set to work. There were so many questions. What had brought her to rebel against her own people in the struggle for Indian independence? How had she managed to endure an Indian jail? What had caused the sea change from wife and mother to Buddhist nun? How and why had she left her children? What drove her? What, if anything, had she sacrificed? What and where were her shadows—those parts of her that may have been hidden behind the glittering, virtuous exterior she presented, and how could I learn about them? And why, exactly, had Lama Yeshe been bowing to her?

In the absence of her physical presence on earth I set out on a journey of discovery, tracing her life through the places she had lived and the people who had known her, to get the answers I sought. It was unusually easy. Everyone I approached was only too willing to tell me their stories and recollections and to give me photographs. That is hardly ever the case, as every writer will tell you. It was as though this book wanted to be written—in spite of myself! Over many months I made several trips to India and talked to nuns, Tibetan government officials, lamas, and laypeople. I met her niece in Bath, England. I traveled to Samye Ling, in Scotland, the first Tibetan monastery in the West to talk to Akong Rinpoche, the lama she had rescued from the refugee camp and brought to live with her in Delhi, who had helped establish the monastery. I had long telephone conversations with people in the United States and Australia.

The most valuable contributors of all, however, were her children. I traveled to Mumbai to meet her second son, Kabir Bedi, the handsome film star. I went to Bangalore to talk to her firstborn, Ranga Bedi, and his wife, Umi. And I flew to the United States to stay with her daughter, Guli, in her lovely lakeside home outside Boston. All were tall, impressive characters—like their mother— with strong personalities, a love of food, and a highly developed sense of humor. Their living memories of their mother, who they unanimously agreed was indeed remarkable, helped bring Freda to life. They also generously handed over her writings, letters, and tape recordings, containing firsthand accounts of her life and thoughts. Precious material indeed. In particular, hearing her voice—clear, firm, measured, full of authority, and highly articulate—was the next best thing to meeting Freda herself.

By the end of my journey, Freda had revealed herself as infinitely bigger, more exciting, and complex than I ever imagined when I set out. The scope of her achievements across a staggering array of different fields was nothing short of extraordinary. Freda's footprint is still very visible in the map of modern India, in the feminist movement, and in the historical march of Buddhism from East to West. Freda was, and is, an icon. I had to concede; the Dalai Lama was right. Freda's story needed to be told.

THE REVOLUTIONARY LIFE OF FREDA BEDI

1

Beginnings

AT FIRST GLANCE, there was little in Freda's beginnings to suggest the exotic life she was to lead, although, as Freda liked to point out, if you looked closely enough, the portents were there from the start. She was born above a small watchmaker's shop in the aptly named Monk Street (hinting at a future life in robes) around the corner from Friary Lane in the heart of old Derby on February 5, 1911. This was England's Midlands—home of Florence Nightingale, Rolls-Royce, and the starkly beautiful Peak District. Snow was falling heavily when Freda came into the world and although she was the firstborn child, her mother birthed her with very little effort. The midwife commented, "Ohhh, Mrs. Houlston, you should be the one to have all the babies, you do it so easily." Freda was a fair-skinned baby, with a perfectly round face, a high forehead, fine wispy hair, and bright blue-gray eyes, inherited from her father who had Norwegian blood coursing through his veins. She was christened Freda Marie Houlston.

Home life for Freda during her first few years was decidedly Dickensian. A photograph of the jeweler's shop shows Freda's father as a small boy, standing outside 28 Monk Street, a typical poor brick, terraced house with a front door opening directly onto the street, with rows of watches hanging in the window like so many baubles. "Houlston" is written large above the lintel. In the doorway is George, Freda's paternal grandfather, in an apron and cloth cap.

Freda, who harbored a romantic streak, remembered it with fondness:

"It was tiny, as attractive to me as the Old Curiosity Shop. I remember my grandmother fussing around in the live-in kitchen, the jewels and the watches in the cabinets. We'd bake bread and cook casseroles in the coal-fired oven, make toast on a toasting fork, wash clothes in a gigantic copper and keep our meat and cheese cold on a stone slab in the larder."

When life inside the tiny shop began to get a little cramped, the family moved to Littleover, a suburb of Derby, on the edge of the countryside, close to Freda's maternal grandmother.

From all accounts hers was a happy, modest, reserved, and decidedly upright family. Her father, Francis ("Frank"), was a tall, strikingly handsome man with an open, honest gaze who cut a dashing figure in his tweed suit and boater. He came from a long line of watchmakers and jewelers, who had all worked in the same tiny shop before him. Francis was deeply religious, a staunch Methodist who favored the teetotalers, and had actually signed the Pledge, the certificate bordered by little homilies: "Look not upon wine, for at last it biteth like a serpent and stingeth like an adder." It stated that Francis Houlston, "with Divine Assistance," would abstain from all alcohol that caused "practices of intemperance." He meant it. Freda recalled him saying that he would never let strong spirits pass his lips even if he were dying and his life depended on it.

Her mother, Nellie, was a stoic woman—tall and straight-backed, with a long face, and her dark hair worn up. She was a stylish woman, and an excellent seamstress who made all of her children's clothes. Nellie had met Frank in the Methodist Chapel of St. Anne's (where her grandparents also worshipped) and was married at age twenty. There was also an element of the adventurer about her, a trait her daughter inherited. Nellie liked to ride around the countryside on a motorbike, play bridge, and at one point was appointed captain of the Mickleover Golf Club, an unusual post for a woman in those days.

Her granddaughter, Pauline Watson, who bears an uncanny resemblance to her aunt Freda, remembers Nellie well. "She was a strong woman, who I found rather formidable. She was very good with money, and held the purse strings. Later on she bought and sold houses. Nellie was also rather psychic, like myself and Freda. It runs in the female line. Nellie got 'feelings' and sensed presences.

She once bought a house but never moved in because she felt unhappy ghosts there," said Pauline, who lives near Bristol, in the United Kingdom.

Freda, who famously never saw ill in anyone, had a distinctly rosy view of her mother. "She had a great altruistic spirit, loving her fellow man. I never knew of anyone near us in need who did not get a helping hand from my mother. Looking back, I think she was a natural bodhisattva, but since she was born in a Christian country, she never encountered the Buddha."

Freda's most interesting family member was her great-grandfather Walker, who as a child had been shipwrecked as he was fleeing France and was plucked from the waves by a preacher named Reverend Walker. Rumor had it that he was the illegitimate son of the Dauphin, although there was no proof. Whatever his ancestry, he did very well, rising from a coach driver to a successful coal contractor. The beautiful pieces of furniture that Nellie eventually inherited came from him.

When Freda was eighteen months old, Frank and Nellie's second child, John, was born. With his blond curly hair and sunny disposition, Freda adored him from the start. They were exceptionally close and maintained a constant correspondence whenever they were apart. "He was a beautiful, strong boy, who inherited the Houlston beauty," she declared. "Believe it or not, we never quarreled." The siblings had very different personalities. Freda was a serious, sensitive, good child, who was rarely seen without a book in her hand. John, on the other hand, was mischievous, fond of playing pranks, and preferred sports to schoolwork. Both, however, had the kindness gene. In adulthood, John joined the philanthropic Christian-based organization Toc H, founded after World War I by Reverend Philip "Tubby" Clayton, to do good works for the sick, elderly, and disadvantaged. Its ethos was example rather than preaching. John was also strongly religious and wanted to enter the Church, but the funds were not available. Instead he opted for the Royal Navy, where he managed to bluff his way into the signals unit in spite of being color-blind. When he died, at age fifty-four from heart disease, the family received hundreds of letters from people expressing how John had helped them. Freda's children reported that when she heard the news, it was the only time they ever saw their mother cry.

By 1914, the clouds of World War I were gathering, threatening not only peace in Europe but the tranquility of the Houlston household.

"The advent of war is very clear in my mind. We were sitting in the drawing room, Mother was pouring tea when there was a great booming sound. It was a bomb that had fallen on Derby station," recalled Freda.

Frank did his duty and joined the Sherwood Foresters as a private in the machine gun corps, and marched off to France. He was killed in the trenches of Aire, on April 14, 1918, just a few weeks before the end of the war. Freda, who was seven years old at the time, was devastated.

"My father's death overshadowed my entire childhood," Freda admitted. "My sadness is that I never really knew him. I have only two vague memories, one of him digging in the garden and the other of him playing with me in the sitting room. I never got the chance to understand him. We had a painting depicting a scene from the English Civil War, in which a child is being questioned about when he had last seen his father. The boy replies, 'I saw him last night in my dreams.' For me it was just like that. To me father is a concept, a sacred concept.

"The Remembrance Day service held annually at a school on November 11 to honor those who had fallen in the War used to open up the wound again and again. I would almost faint with grief," she said.

She later revealed that her father's death opened her up to the pain and suffering experienced by all humans everywhere, preparing her for the Buddhist path. The Truth of Universal Suffering was the first of the Buddha's Four Noble Truths—his seminal doctrine, outlining the path to liberation.

Nellie, who had seen her husband's death when he appeared at the foot of her bed one morning, five days before the telegram arrived, suffered a near-collapse, but carried on. When she recovered, she announced, quite firmly, that she would never set foot in church again, on the grounds that she could no longer believe in a God who could take someone as good as her husband or separate a wife from the husband she loved so much. She later married another Frank, Francis Swann, a railway clerk, the youngest of eleven, who lived with three spinster sisters not far from Nellie. Freda was the first to concede it was not a marriage of young lovers.

"Frank Swann was thirty-five, and it occurred to him that it would be a good idea to marry the young widow—it was a union of two people who had decided they would like to spend the rest of their lives together. My second father was a good-natured, kindly man, who followed his own interests (mainly amateur dramatics), and who never interfered with our upbringing."

The second drama of Freda's childhood occurred when she contracted diphtheria at age eleven. An epidemic was sweeping the country, killing many children. Penicillin had not yet been invented, and Freda grew increasingly weak. Seeing that her daughter was dying, Nellie followed her intuition and took her to a doctor in Nottingham, who prescribed putting her in a tent in the garden. Curiously, the unorthodox treatment worked.

"He must have been a genius doctor because, under the beech tree and by the laburnum, I was soon on my way to recovery," Freda wrote in her notebook. From that day on Freda had a predilection for tents, and at every opportunity would dive into them, taking her children with her—be it in the high, remote foothills of the Himalayas or in strange dirt parks in Delhi. In her journals she attributed her love of canvas to a previous life as a nomad in Tibet, as she did her empathy with the surrounding countryside she grew up in.

"I loved the stark Derbyshire landscape. There is a mysterious, esoteric quality about it—the black rock forms, close-cropped grass, walls of stone like the *mani* stone I saw in Tibet. No other English county is like it, except maybe Cornwall," she wrote.

Freda and John spent hours roaming freely over the Derbyshire hills and dales, collecting mushrooms and blackberries, making daisy chains. They wandered through bluebell woods, explored the magical Sherwood Forest (Robin Hood's hideaway) and visited

Derby's great old stately homes, such as Pemberley, now a pilgrim-age site for devotees of Mr. Darcy, hero of Jane Austen's *Pride and Prejudice*. And they bought bowls of fresh butter from the small farms dotted over the countryside.

"We were very happy," she said simply. Freda's love of nature, which bordered on pantheism, never left her. It informed her poetry, her writings, her very soul, and she would wax lyrical whenever she spoke of it. "I recall the exquisite perfume of the lilac tree outside the kitchen door, and the pear tree with its blossoms tumbling over the garden wall in the magical days of spring."

It was an unspoiled, ordered childhood of a bygone age.

Nellie would sew; preserve fruits and vegetables; make jams, pickles, and herb root beer. The only entertainment was a crystal radio, brought into the house when Freda was eleven. They would gather around it in the evening, prodding it with a contraption called the "cat's whisker" to find the sensitive spot to make it spring to life.

During her formative years, Freda nurtured the innate spiritual side of her nature that was to persist and grow until it dominated her entire existence. She described its development this way: "I was a Christian brought up in a Christian family. My mother may have turned her back on God, but she sent me to Sunday school and then to church because she thought her husband would have wanted it. My godmother, Auntie Lilly, loved me dearly, and was a quiet influence with a quality of joy. She used to play me hymns."

It was her confirmation, at age fourteen, at St. Peter's Church, Littleover, that truly opened the spiritual door. "When I took Holy Communion, I felt there was something different there—a direct communication, a sense of awe in the face of the Divine," she said. Her minister, whom she called Brown Owl on account of his spectacles and hooked nose, was wary. "He saw I was more interested in Mass than most girls and warned my mother that she should keep an eye on me. That was a typical attitude of the Church of England then, which was obsessed with fetes, and meetings, and showed an utter lack of understanding of anything connected to the spiritual life in its deepest sense."

It triggered a deep-seated yearning that was to last all her life. As always Freda turned to books to find out what this yearning was, and what it meant. "I read the Anglo Catholic writers, and the biographies of the saints. The life story of Saint Thérèse of Carmel, the book of Saint John of the Cross, trying to find out how they had reached this exalted state. It was a turning point. I discovered all these saints of the past had sought Reality, the Truth, and were not satisfied until they had reached some direct intuition of the Light, the life in the cosmos. This started a new stream of thought. If they can do it, why can't I sit quietly and contemplate."

Freda had discovered that what she was looking for could not be found in dogma but only through going within. "I realized that Brown Owl's sermons and all the things that went on in the Church had no meaning for me at all," she said.

There was no one nearby to help her. England in the 1920s had not even heard of meditation. Christmas Humphreys, a judge and scholar, opened the first Buddhist Society in 1926, at Eccleston Square, London, based primarily in Zen. The Theosophists had thought about things Buddhist, but nothing had percolated through to provincial libraries, schools, or homes.

Freda was not only sincere, she was extraordinarily determined —unusual traits for a girl that young. "The only thing I could think of was to go to church when nobody was there. I used to slip away from home in the early hours before school, sit alone in the pews, and just wait. There was always a prayer in my heart to reach God, or whatever you call that power or love beyond thought. I was only deeply interested in what I could find out from direct, intuitive understanding."

She had taken the first step of the spiritual seeker, setting out on a journey that was to last nearly forty years, when she eventually found the path that she was looking for.

In the meantime she kept her head in books. There were hints in her choice of reading of where she was heading. "Whenever anything from the East came into my hands—poetry, literature of any sort—there was always more than an ordinary depth of response," she said.

2

Expanding World

FREDA WAS DRIVEN as much by her brain as by her innate
spiritual impulses. She was known as a clever and studious girl
who excelled at her lessons. She attended the newly opened Parkfields Cedars, established on Kedleston Road in 1917, which had as
its guiding motto "To Produce Girls of Distinction." Freda loved it.
She described in glowing terms its rolling lawns, magnificent oak
paneling, sweeping staircase, well-equipped library, stately cedar
trees, and dedicated unmarried staff, "living for their work and loving the children. I can still see the head, Miss Kay, a Scot, who was
a rather strong, bulldog-looking type, with the winter sun stream-
ing in behind her, illuminating her white hair as she said morning
prayers. She had an unsentimental way with the Bible, especially
the Old Testament and the psalms of David. Beside her was one picture, Botticelli's 'Annunciation.' Morning prayers were a time of joy
for me."

Freda eventually became "head girl," a student leader who served
as the official representative of the school. "We knew that she was
brainy, completely into books," said Pauline Watson, Freda's niece.
"When I visited one of her school friends, she told me that Freda
was not like most of them—she wasn't interested in parties or boy-
friends. She had her goals and went toward them."

This was 1920s postwar Britain, and while most young girls were
amusing themselves with flappers, fringes, and frivolity, Freda was
content with ballroom dancing, arts and crafts, and following her
mother around the golf course, the only sport that interested her.
She loathed swimming in the local baths but was grateful that she
had learned how to swim, because swimming in the lakes of Kashmir gave her hours of pleasure later in her life.

But it was in her schoolwork that she excelled, especially literature and languages. It helped that she had a photographic memory,
a fact that she made little of. One teacher in particular, Miss Glass,
earned her lifelong gratitude for teaching her French. Freda had
a particular aptitude for the language, owing, she thought, to her
mysterious French maternal great-grandfather.

"Whether it came from my great-grandfather or not, Miss Glass
recognized and encouraged my special talent for French, lend-
ing me books, getting me to the stage where I could read rapidly,
and giving me a great appreciation for French literature. All that I
achieved in French got me to Oxford, and was due to her. I can't be
grateful enough," she said. "The story of my childhood is all about
developing myself to the point, whether consciously or not, where I
could be admitted to Oxford University."

In spite of her natural cleverness, university had not originally
been on Freda's agenda, especially not Oxford. She was never ambitious in that way, and had assumed that she would stay in Derbyshire
and lead a quiet, domesticated if industrious life, like her mother.
It was a masterstroke of fate that determined Freda's future and it
came in the form of Elsie Ludlow, a school friend whose Quaker
family wanted her to get into Oxford.

"Elsie was an enterprising girl, but not very bright. She asked me
if I would study with her for the entrance exam, because she knew
she wouldn't have the incentive to do it by herself. On the spur of
the moment, I took the exam with her, without much preparation
at all. To my great surprise I was called for an interview, though
Elsie wasn't. I was told I had a good chance of getting in the following year, to read French, if I brushed up on my language skills."

Nine months spent living with her French pen pal in Reims and
attending the local school did the trick. Although Freda confessed
she didn't actually like the sound and pitch of the French voice—she
said it got on her nerves—when she next took the Oxford exam, her
new French accent helped her pass. It was an extraordinary achievement, but one that was still tantalizingly out of reach. Her family
simply did not have the money. Undeterred, Freda set her sights on
winning a scholarship. Competition was stiff for England's oldest,
most prestigious university—with only twelve places being allotted

out of three hundred applicants, but Freda succeeded. She received the news with remarkable equanimity.

"One day I got a letter saying that I had been awarded an 'exhibition' for St. Hugh's College, Oxford. I really had no idea what it meant. In fact it was a scholarship worth so much money per month. I put the letter in my pocket and set off to school on the Huddleston Road tram." As it happened, Miss Glass, her French teacher, was sitting at the other end. "When we reached the Parkfields Cedars stop, I took the letter out and showed her. She looked at me in an unbelieving way and said in a shaking voice, 'You mean you've sat there on the tram all this time without rushing up to tell me?'" It was indicative of Freda's very calm, controlled, unemotional response to the dramatic things that life presented her.

At Parkfields Cedars, Freda was hailed as the first girl to get into Oxford, and with an exhibition at that. But still Freda was far from being able to go. She now had the money for the fees but not enough for the boarding and living costs. Again, with the encouragement of Miss Glass, she put her mind to getting two further scholarships, one from the county and the other from the state—both of which she duly won. "Finally there was enough money for three terms plus thirty-three pounds in pocket money. My mother would provide me with the clothes I needed."

In the autumn of 1929, a naïve eighteen-year-old Freda traveled by train, tram, and bicycle to St. Hugh's, one of Oxford's prettiest colleges, founded by Elizabeth Wordsworth (great-niece of the poet William Wordsworth) specifically for girls of modest means. It was strictly segregated. St. Hugh's was one of only three women's colleges, Oxford being a bastion of male privilege where women's degrees were not even legally recognized until 1920. Nevertheless, St. Hugh's had rapidly developed a reputation for producing women of unusual radical and determined character. Men were not admitted until 1986.

"It was a very quiet little student who came up to St. Hugh's and wore the long exhibition gown to the lectures," Freda conceded. Oxford opened the doors of the world to her. At St. Hugh's she drew to her a small group of girls who were to go on to become some of the most powerful figures of their time. They stayed friends for years. From this time on, Freda was to mingle effortlessly with the great and the good from all cultures and ways of life.

Leading the pack was the inimitable, feisty Barbara Betts, later better known as Barbara Castle, the first woman to become First Secretary of State under Prime Minister Harold Wilson, and hailed as one of the most important Labor politicians of the twentieth century. She was a major influence on Freda's life, steering her away from her provincial upbringing into an infinitely bolder, more sophisticated life.

"Barbara brought with her a flavor of the north of England, where I was brought up, as well as the sturdy atmosphere of the great pioneers of English socialism," commented Freda. There was also Olive Salt Gorton, who became a pillar of the BBC and broke down class barriers by introducing regional accents to the airwaves to balance the clipped tones of "received pronunciation." "Olive brought the people of England into the BBC with programs like 'Underneath the Arches.' She took the microphone onto the pavements." And there was Olive Chandler, whom Freda was particularly fond of and with whom she maintained a lifelong correspondence: "She was a quiet little nun of a girl with a dove-like quality who was like my good conscience. When she saw me getting too excited with outside activities, she used to bring me back to my books and look after me." While Freda was appraising her friends, they also had their opinion of her, summed up by Barbara Castle in her autobiography, *Fighting All the Way*:

"The third member of our triumvirate was Freda Houlston, a dark, strikingly attractive girl who came from a modest, middle-class family whose conventional values Mrs. Thatcher would have approved of," wrote the dyed-in-the-wool socialist somewhat scathingly of her archrival, the deeply conservative Margaret Thatcher. "Freda was not as lighthearted as Olive and I were, alternating between bursts of gaiety and moods of deep and almost somber seriousness."

Freda threw herself into her new world with great energy. She reveled in the sheer beauty and historical grandeur of the place—

Shakespeare on the lawn, fireflies on balmy summer evenings by the River Isis, romantic May balls. She joined just about every society, from the League of Nations to the Ornithological Club. And over cups of cocoa, she talked long into the night with her coterie of like-minded friends on the usual student subjects: literature, travel, politics, and sex—the latter instigated by Barbara Castle, who was fervent in her campaign to shed the shackles of Victorian prudery, repression, and ignorance. She organized a whip-round, where everyone puts in money, to buy *Parenthood: Design or Accident?*, Michael Fielding's groundbreaking book, complete with explicit drawings, which became exceptionally well thumbed.

It was not enough to divert Freda from her studies, however. She worked hard for "responsions," the first-year exams, which consisted of a curious mix of topics ranging from Logic through Virgil's *Aeneid*, aimed at preparing her for the following two years of French, old and new. Freda breezed through them, but her heart had gone out of her chosen subject. Her world had expanded too far.

"Suddenly I couldn't be bothered," she said. "I wanted to learn other languages, and History, Modern Philosophy, and International and Colonial Politics. I wanted to understand the world! I had this flash of understanding that French, Ancient and Modern, could only lead to me being a teacher. I passionately did *not* want to go back into the world of childhood."

She began to set her sights on the infinitely tougher and more sophisticated world of journalism. She aimed for the top.

"I wanted to interpret the incredible international adult world that poured out of magazines and newspapers. My idea was to work my way up from cub reporter on the *Derby Telegraph* to Fleet Street, home of Britain's prestigious national press." With Barbara Castle's encouragement, Freda dropped French and took up Modern Greats (Philosophy, Politics, and Economics).

Oxford may have been idyllic at that time, but outside its hallowed halls life was grim for most people. The year 1929 heralded the start of the Great Depression, the biggest economic downturn

Great Britain had ever experienced. Unemployment, poverty, and hunger stalked the land. Sensitized to pain and suffering by her father's death, Freda grew increasingly uneasy with the disparity of her privileged life in contrast to the hardships of others. Oxford, heartland of the Establishment, was where the class system reached its zenith.

"There was an underlying sense of guilt in the face of the reality of the economic conditions. We *cared* that people hadn't got enough food, we *cared* that there were hunger marches, we *cared* that children in slums were starving. It's impossible for people now to understand, in these relatively prosperous times, the stark division that existed between Right and Left. The Right wanted nothing to change. They wanted life to go on the way it had before World War I. The idealism of the people I was mixing with was that of helping the underprivileged. But what can one do at university except talk?" she said.

Inevitably, like many Oxbridge intellectuals of her day, she became increasingly left wing, joined the Labor Club along with Barbara Castle and Michael Foot (the future Labor prime minister), and began to class herself as one of the "Burning Socialists." She meant it. Freda's idealism about a fairer world never left her. From Oxford on, she fought a tireless campaign against social, legal, economic, gender, racial, class, and eventually religious inequality wherever she found it.

She was inspired and fired up on her quest by the impressive lineup of exceptional, world-renowned thinkers of her day, all Oxford professors, whose eloquent arguments filled the lecture halls to overflowing: Harold Laski, professor of Political Science, who specialized in Karl Marx; Keir Hardie, the great constitutionalist and pacifist, who was one of the founders of the Labor Party; Ephraim Lipson, author of *The Economic History of England*; and Professor Sir Alfred Zimmern, whose name is associated with the founding of the League of Nations. He later became a close personal friend of Freda and her husband.

"My belief in the charter of human rights was very strong, so that

I saw Marxism not as a cheap political stunt, but in a deep, direct way." Freda rapidly learned German in order to be able to read and study Hegel, Marx, and the German philosophers in the original.

Her spiritual life was not forgotten, however, and was running smoothly along parallel lines. Every Sunday she went to church to take Communion and would pop into chapel if there was Bach concert. Any hint of Eastern thought drew her like a magnet. She devoured *The Light of Asia*, subtitled *The Great Renunciation*, by Sir Edwin Arnold—an epic poem describing the life of Prince Siddhartha, who became the Buddha. And she rushed to attend a lecture by Rabindranath Tagore, the Bengali Nobel Prize–winning poet, philosopher, songwriter, and educator, and was immediately entranced.

"I first saw him at Oxford lecturing on the highest philosophy before some of the greatest savants and philosophers in the West. He sat on a low platform with the rare light of the late evening falling on his face and making a complete aureole around his white head. I was very moved by his understanding, his dignity, the way in which he seemed to distill the essence of India into the small hall and with it the essence of all that is highest and universal in man. At that time my knowledge of India was superficial and I did not know it was to be my home, but my response to Tagore and what he was saying was immediate. I believe that Tagore, more than any other Indian, has been able to interpret the East, and her aspirations, and make them understood in the West. He was often obtuse and above the mind of ordinary man, but something in the very radiance of his presence did more than the words of popular speakers. Tagore's heart was one with both the old and the renascent India, and though not a politician he could not keep silent in the face of the great outrage of Fascism and war."

The other great Indian she encountered was Mahatma Gandhi, who gave two talks at Oxford on October 24, 1931. His avowed intent was "to realize the dream of my life—the freedom of my country." His method was peaceful revolution. Freda listened hard.

3

Love

L IFE AT OXFORD was not all socialism and study, however.
Freda was not the flirty, flighty type, and she never escaped
over the wall into town for dances without the required late pass,
like her more rebellious friends, Barbara Castle and Olive Shapley.
But she was not beyond love. One day she was unusually early for a
lecture and found a young Indian man, also atypically early, leaning
against a wall reading a paper. There were several Indian students
at Oxford, but in the 1930s, racial discrimination was strong.

"I thought I'd better say good morning or else he'll think I was
snubbing him. I made some remark about the day's news, and the
young man just muttered good morning in reply and went back to
his reading," recalled Freda. Later, the young Indian thought the
beautiful tall woman who had spoken to him must have thought
he was a complete boor, and to make amends for his rudeness, he
invited her to tea.

Freda was surprised, but accepted, having duly engaged a chaperone to accompany her, following college rules, which stipulated
that young ladies should not visit the rooms of the opposite sex
alone. That was the start of an immediate affinity and later a passionate love affair.

His full name was Baba Phyare Lal Bedi, (shortened to BPL or
plain Bedi by Freda), a Sikh from the Punjab. He was a giant of a
man, the All India Hammer-Throwing Champion, with a round
face, mustache, and wavy black hair. His background was infinitely
more illustrious than Freda's. He was the sixteenth direct descendant of Guru Nanak (1469–1539), founder of the Sikh religion,
whose family still lived on the ancestral lands owned by Guru

Nanak himself. Within Indian circles this classified him virtually as "royal." BPL came from a long line of lawyers and was at Oxford on a Half Blue scholarship (awarded to athletes of outstanding ability) studying Modern Greats.

BPL had a booming voice, a larger-than-life personality, and loved nothing more than good company, good jokes, and especially good food.

"Unorthodox is one word to describe my father. He was a born rebel, one of the big Lefties of his time," says Kabir Bedi, Freda's second child and a Bollywood legend. "Apart from his enormous strength—at school he was always the anchor in the tug-of-war competitions—he was famous for eating. He loved food. He would demolish a whole basket of boiled eggs on the way to school as if they were almonds. Once, a family friend, a hunter, sent over a whole deer that he had shot and cooked. My father and his brother, then both in their teens, decided to tackle the meat. Their mother was furious and said they would be severely beaten if they didn't eat it all. They ate and ate, and fearing the inevitable thrashing, threw great slabs of the venison into the neighbor's garden to get rid of it. Even the young Bedi boys couldn't finish an entire deer. Well, the neighbor was a Jain, totally vegetarian and furious. The ensuing argument was never forgotten.

"With his own children, he was the most indulgent father you could find. He was a real softie. Mummy was the disciplinarian. My father more or less let us do what we liked. I hated school and I remember, when Mummy was away, he would say, 'It's OK, leave the house as though you're going to school and just run away on the way there.'"

Superficially, they seemed an unlikely couple. BPL was quixotic and loud. Freda was refined and contained. They became known as Beauty and the Beast, but they soon found common ground.

"At tea, I found him to be a warm man with an interesting mind, and we quickly became friends," Freda wrote, with typical reserve.

Initially the glue was their shared admiration of communism and socialist ideals, so fashionable among the Oxbridge intellectuals of their day, who were eager to build a better, fresher world after the devastation of World War I. Cambridge, in particular, became a famous, well-documented breeding ground for communist gentlemen spies. Revolution was in the air, first in Russia then in China, overthrowing the old order, making way for the new. It was exhilarating. The Suffragettes were on the march too, chaining themselves to rails, throwing themselves under horses, and going on hunger strikes to obtain equal rights with men. The atmosphere was electric.

Freda, reading Marx in the original, could not help but be moved by his arguments for championing the oppressed, the exploited, the downtrodden, and the poor. She had personally seen children in the slums in Derby running around with bare feet, undernourished babies in the hands of incompetent mothers, and of course knew of the hunger marches of the unemployed. To her caring nature, Marxism symbolized humanism, justice, and ultimately freedom. These were causes she could and would readily dedicate her life to.

What they both recognized was the approaching menace of fascism, with its anti-Semitic agenda, which to them was anathema. Only communism, they believed, was strong and brave enough to oppose and defeat it. While their government, loath to take up arms again, was talking appeasement, only the communists and Christians seemed to understand the danger of what Hitler and Mussolini were wanting to bring about—and were willing to go to jail for saying it.

Of course the young Oxford idealists did not know then of the gulags, the terrible persecutions, the appalling death toll, the insane economic policies that killed millions, and the sheer tyranny that communist rule evoked. Nor did they comprehend the utter lack of freedom of thought, speech, and belief—the very things that Freda and BPL held most dear—that ensued.

In the heady days of the early 1930s, Freda and BPL were enthusiastically having tea in town, and meeting at lectures and the Bodleian Library to discuss their ideals. In time, Freda went openly to BPL's rooms to talk and work without the chaperone. Deciding they had to do something to start bringing about the change they wanted, they sat down together and compiled a book on Marx's letters. When that was done, they went on to edit three volumes of contemporary Indian economic, social, and international writings, entitled *India Analysed*, which was later published by Victor Gollancz. Freda was just twenty and BPL was twenty-two.

Inevitably, Freda was increasingly drawn into Bedi's Indian world—and she loved everything about it. He introduced her to his cuisine (unsurprisingly he was an excellent cook) and took her to the Matji, the very noisy mock Indian parliament, which staged disorderly debates. The students she met there became good friends and leading figures in the new India: Vidyar Shankar, the right-hand man of Sardar Patel; Humayun Kabir, an enlightened administrator; Lakshmanan, first Indian director of All India Radio; writer and poet Mahmud-u-Zaffar, also called Mahmud Saheb Zada Bane, among many others.

"It was an interesting time, and somehow all this turmoil of the Indian independence movement, and the students who were ready to dedicate their lives to it, entered my own life in a very natural way. I began to feel for India and her people even while living in Oxford," she said.

Most of all, however, BPL talked to Freda about his one overriding mission and intent—to free India from British rule. Imperialism was part of the repugnant old order that had to be overthrown, and he was determined to help bring it about. Under the Bedi family motto, "Honesty and Justice," he was convinced he would succeed. Freda was more than sympathetic. She loved her country, she said, but she loathed imperialism.

It was not only politics over which they bonded; they also found affinity in their spiritual orientation. Oxford, with its intellectual liberalism and vast library, provided Freda with a wider scope of religious inquiry. Hearing Gandhi and Tagore and listening to BPL opened her up to Eastern beliefs. Her spiritual horizons were broadening considerably.

"I decided completely that my search for Truth was beyond the Church, beyond Christianity even. By now I had become conscious of all the religions in the world. At Oxford, I realized I wanted to follow the path of the seeker, and the path of the meditator," she said.

BPL understood that. Although he belonged to the Sikh Guru family, he himself was not orthodox. "He did not attach himself to any particular religion, but to all gurus and those who believe in deeper truths. This of course included his devotion to his ancestor, Guru Nanak, which was very great."

At one point, Freda showed him a drawing she had done when she was seven. "You've drawn the Lord Buddha," BPL told her. He later added, "It explained why she was drawn to India, and why she fit in so well, and her great attachment to Buddhism in the latter part of her life. Everything that happened to her was the inheritance of a past life. Her karma was there from the very start."

Her love affair with the hammer-throwing champion and his country had begun. For Freda this was both thrilling and terrifying. In 1920, falling in love with an Indian was a bold and risky move. Racial prejudice was ubiquitous; notices outside boarding houses announced, "No Dogs, Jews, or Coloreds"; blacks were regularly spat at, shunned, and beaten up. The prejudice wasn't all one way, either; to many upper-class Indians their greatest fear in sending their precious sons overseas to be educated was that they would end up "marrying the landlady's daughter."

For whatever reasons, Freda was unusually free from such prejudice. She openly began to be seen with Bedi, and the young mixed-race couple paid a heavy price. BPL was targeted by fellow students more than once—though the assailants came off worse. Freda was shunned by her peers, although her closest friends rallied round and tried to protect her from the barbs. Finally an officious school doorman porter, traditionally in charge of the comings and goings of the students, reported Freda to the authorities for going to BPL's room unaccompanied. The result was that Freda was suspended for the rest of the academic year.

"It was nonsense," snorted Freda. "Everyone was going into each other's rooms and no one else was reported. Because I was white and BPL was Indian, I had to suffer the indignity of being suspended. It really brought me up against the question of racial discrimination. The suffering we both underwent—BPL because he thought he was the cause of it—only brought us closer together," she added defiantly.

But underneath the sensitivity, Freda was a stoic young woman with a strong spirit. Her friend Barbara Castle said that on Freda's return to school, "she resumed her visits to Bedi, in the digs outside college where he had moved, only this time she decided to give the disciplinarians their money's worth and started an affair with him."

Still, the trauma and tension of sticking to her principles took its toll. Freda suffered a nervous breakdown, which meant she had to leave school for another term. But her love for Bedi grew stronger and endured. When she recovered, Freda returned to Oxford to finish her degree. BPL in turn decided enough was enough and proposed.

"I have nothing to offer you but love and this companionship that I think we both feel," he said. "I am a member of the Indian National Movement and a follower of Gandhi. For all I know, you might have to spend the years of our marriage waiting outside jail walls." He did not know how prophetic his words would turn out to be.

Freda remembered, "I never thought about it twice. I said, 'Yes, whatever the future brings, we will share it together.'" In saying yes to BPL, Freda was in effect agreeing to become an outlaw to her own country, to go against its rule. She had joined the revolution.

Many years later, in conversation with her children, she likened herself to Marie Curie, who had agreed to marry for much the same reason. Marie herself had said of her relationship with Pierre, "An extraordinary romance unfolded. He spoke to me of his dream of an existence consecrated entirely to scientific research—and asked me to share that life."

The similarities did not stop there, however. Marie, like Freda, had been devoted to her cause, was obsessed by her work (at the expense of her children), and had a deep-seated urge to help. She single-handedly saved hundreds of soldiers during the World War I with her mobile X-ray units. She was also brilliant, brave, single-minded, and the ultimate high-achiever, having won two Nobel Prizes, the first for physics, which she shared with her husband, the second on her own terms, for chemistry in 1911, the year of Freda's birth.

If BPL thought that marriage would mollify the prudes and racists, he was terribly mistaken. News of their engagement unleashed a tsunami of outrage that went far beyond the Oxford establishment all the way to Parliament. Theirs was to be the first marriage of a white Oxford undergraduate to a nonwhite student. The Establishment—those bodies in power who protect the status quo—quaked in fear and anger, recalling that only the year before, Edwina Mountbatten, the wife of the viceroy of India, had been forced to bring a libel suit against a publication for alleging she'd had an affair with a black man, generally thought to be American actor Paul Robeson.

"The controversy went all the way to London, where a Round Table Conference was being held with Mahatma Gandhi and a great many of India's senior statesmen," said Freda. "We were told by friends that Rangaswami Iyengar, the Indian journalist, lawyer, and politician had staunchly supported us. 'Why shouldn't our boys marry the best English girls? Why should they have to marry girls who are not at university?' he argued. Hearing that, we went up to London to thank him."

The next hurdle for Freda was breaking the news to her mother. It was, in her words, "traumatic." Marrying BPL meant leaving England for good, and since sea voyages were the only means of travel, the chances of seeing her mother again were slim.

She had taken BPL to meet her mother, and BPL had tried to endear himself by taking her a present of golf balls, since she was by now a champion. But although the encounter was pleasant, it wasn't warm. Mrs. Swann was conservative, and BPL was the total opposite. BPL was never truly friendly with his mother-in-law.

"I remember I had a terrible toothache on the day I decided to tell my mother. That morning I went to the dentist with what I was going to do all bottled up inside me. He gave me gas, but it wouldn't work. 'You must have something big on your mind, because you are fighting the anesthetic and it won't work properly. I can't take the tooth out,' he said. I went home with the tooth still in and faced my mother. She was at the kitchen sink washing the dishes when I told her I was going to marry BPL. She went very quiet and then said, 'I trust you and your judgment and I know you would not marry a bad man, but I am really sorry you are leaving.'"

Barbara Castle, on the other hand, was delighted. "Thank heavens," she said. "I was afraid you were going to become a dull little suburban housewife."

All went smoothly after that except for one incident that almost caused the wedding to be canceled. "Father came from a very male-dominated world," Kabir told me, "and he asked Mummy to peel an orange for him. 'Why don't you peel your own orange?' snapped my independent-minded mother. This was an insufferable affront to Baba's male pride, and they had a huge argument. It escalated into a real issue, until finally they reached a compromise: Mummy would peel oranges for him, but he would not begin to eat until she had peeled her own."

Freda married BPL on June 12, 1933, at the Oxford Registrar's Office. She was twenty-two and he was twenty-six.

"It was a low-key affair. After finishing lectures we called my mother and stepfather, and BPL called his cousin, Kuldip Bedi, to act as witnesses. The ceremony was simple, in the drab registry office, and afterward we had a very ordinary wedding breakfast. Neither of us wanted a big party or any fuss," said Freda.

The local newspaper covered the event—after all, this was a "first." It was just the beginning of many firsts Freda clocked up. The photograph in the paper shows a smiling groom gallantly holding an umbrella over his bride, who looks demurely beautiful in a long white dress with frilled short sleeves, a large bow at the back, white gloves, and a small corsage of flowers clipped to her bodice.

They were the last Western clothes she ever wore. From her marriage onward she happily wore Indian dress, in which she stated she felt perfectly at home. "From my wedding day onward I thought of myself as Indian," she stated. The metamorphosis from provincial Derbyshire girl to cosmopolitan, politically-aware Indian bride was complete. Their honeymoon was also unorthodox—a camping tour of Europe with a Ugandan Indian friend, who owned the car. "Touring and tents! What could be better?" she enthused.

Their creative, radical Oxford days were over. Both Freda and

BPL received their degrees and a whole new life beckoned. It was not what Freda had imagined. She had successfully lined up a job as a cub reporter on the *Derby Telegraph*, her first stepping-stone to Fleet Street (as she had intended). Instead she went to Germany with her new husband, who had won a Humboldt scholarship at the Friedrich Wilhelm University in Berlin, to research a PhD in Political Science.

"Bedi was concerned about the rise of Hitler, but he thought that as long as he didn't get a chance to rant in Parliament, it would be all right. He was going to keep a very keen eye on the situation," she said. She was not to see her homeland again for fourteen years.

4

Transitions

B Y THE TIME Freda reached Berlin, she was pregnant, and delighted with the prospect of motherhood. BPL somewhat protectively decided that she should not work, but instead live quietly in the charming little cottage they had found on the bank of Lake Wannsee. "It was really a lovely place, with a beautiful garden, and we had some very happy months there preparing for the child," she said. She busied herself with making baby clothes, but could not resist going to Berlin University to study Hindi with a Punjabi professor—a necessary preparation, she thought, for a life on the subcontinent, and to counteract the full-on domesticity she found herself in.

As a new bride with a baby coming and living in a foreign land, Freda missed her mother enormously, but was comforted by the presents she received from BPL's mother, Bhabooji, whom she grew to love dearly.

"She was a widow who, after her husband's death, had gone to live with her own very enlightened family in the state of Pusla. Naturally the idea that her son had married a foreigner must have been rather a shock. With typical diplomacy, however, she accepted the situation and sent very beautiful clothes for the baby and also for me—saris and blouses—as well as delicacies that she thought her son must have missed while abroad. He always had a great time getting these food packages through customs. He once made the customs officer sample one of the really dry dal cakes to prove that it couldn't be sold in Germany. Bhabooji was an extraordinary woman. I used to think of her as a great patriot."

BPL refrained from any political activity in Germany, although he was keeping up-to-date with the Free India movement in India. A frequent visitor to their lakeside cottage was Subhas Chandra Bose, who went on to become one of the most prominent and controversial leaders of the independence movement. Bose was educated at Cambridge and also had a European wife—Emilie Schenkl, an Austrian. He made it a point to visit sympathetic Indian students living in Europe, and the couple had much in common with Freda and BPL Bedi.

"We came to know Bose intimately, and a deep friendship grew," said BPL. Bose was a hard-core communist, a great admirer of the Soviet Union, who maintained that only an authoritarian state, not democracy, would be able to reshape India. (Later he was forced to resign as president of the Indian National Congress because his platform of violent resistance clashed with Gandhi's peaceful pathway.)

In Germany, however, Bose, won the young BPL over completely. "Freda and I were both fired up with the patriotic zeal of liberating the motherland from British imperialism," BPL said. "While we were in Berlin, an eminent journalist asked me what was my agenda for India. 'Live dangerously,' I replied. 'Live dangerously for every form of exploitation of man by man. Live dangerously for every form of injustice. Live dangerously for any violation of human dignity.'"

On May 13, 1934, Freda gave birth to a son after just a four-hour labor. The baby weighed eight pounds and was perfectly healthy; Freda and BPL were besotted. "He seemed to me the most beautiful baby in the whole world—that goes without saying! He had rosy cheeks, a little cap of dark hair, and the most astoundingly beautiful eyelashes," wrote Freda. They named him Ranga after the Indian statesman who had defeated the political opposition to their marriage, ten months previously.

Nazism was all around, but Freda, wrapped up in motherhood, seemed blissfully unaware. "I was coming back from the market one day with some beautiful Jaffa oranges, which I presented to my landlady. She turned up her nose and said, 'I don't eat Jewish fruit.' That's when I found out she was a Nazi. I'd had no idea."

BPL had not joined any political club at Berlin University, nor was he taking part in any political activities, but he sensed that tension was mounting. He was friendly with many of the Indian students living in the International Houses, which were being increasingly dominated by Nazi representatives.

In August 1934, Hitler was made führer. The morning the news broke, BPL put down his paper and announced, "Tomorrow we get on the train and go to Geneva. It's not safe here anymore."

"He knew that Hitler could swoop down on the Indian students, which was precisely what happened," said Freda. The life of drama and danger that she pledged to share with Bedi had begun. "You can imagine the state I was in, having to pack up everything in one day, and with BPL having to get the visas for Switzerland. But the next morning we were on the train!" she said.

After their hasty exit, they spent a few pleasant weeks staying in accommodations that had been arranged by their old Oxford professor, Alfred Zimmern, who ran a school there. In October 1934, they finally made the decision to go to India and make it their permanent home. They sailed on the SS *Conte Verde* from northern Italy to Bombay, a journey of three weeks. Freda found the experience horrifying: She had to negotiate thousands of cockroaches on her way to the ship's kitchen to get the milk she needed to nourish herself while she was breast-feeding Ranga. Her aversion to dirt and grime never left her. For the rest of her life in India she carried a wash-bag whenever she traveled, and refused to eat at roadside stalls. Her entry into India itself was not more welcoming. News of their political activities and pro-Independence stance in London had reached the authorities, and they were subjected to body searches. "Even little Ranga's diaper was taken off and searched. Really, it was just too much," she declared.

An indignant, bedraggled Freda arrived in the Punjab, homeland of the Sikhs, after an exhausting two-day train journey wearing a dirty white cotton sari and carrying baby Ranga in a little French sailor suit, which to Freda "looked quite adorable." She was met by Bhabooji, who was wearing the classic dress of the widow— white veil and kurta with black trousers—and BPL taught her how to touch his mother's feet in the traditional way of respect. Because it was BPL's mother, Freda was happy to oblige.

There followed an exceptionally warm and affectionate welcome as the Bedi family followed the age-old rituals of bringing the bride into the groom's house. The grandfather gave Freda the traditional Rs 11, Bhabooji placed a traditional red dupatta (a scarf-like cloth) around her shoulders, and the whole family poured gifts onto a red veil that had been placed on the ground. The state band was brought in, and played extremely loud music, and endless family delicacies were served. It was a stark contrast to the drab wedding ceremony they'd had in Oxford. Freda was presented with clean, beautiful saris, and Bhabooji tactfully persuaded Freda to get Ranga out of his sailor suit by giving him kurtas, the collarless muslin shirts, on the grounds they would offer more protection from the sun. "The whole event was very beautiful. Most importantly, there was no trace of racial antagonism," said Freda.

It could well have been so very different. Freda was a daughter of the British Empire, the greatest empire the world had ever known, four times larger than that of ancient Rome, governing one-fifth of humanity. It also was a commercial superpower, boasting the mightiest naval and military force ever seen. India was the jewel in their glittering crown. If you were born English, you were on the top rung of life, and Freda had gone one better. She was a graduate of the oldest, most prestigious English university, a woman of stature, fresh off the boat. In the society of "them and us," Indians were all too used to the haughty, superior ways of the memsahibs bossing them around—and they were beginning to resent them.

To their delight, Freda was nothing like that. She wore a sari, and she tried to speak to them in their own language. "That really knocked them out. Learning Hindi was her biggest coup de grâce," said Kabir. "From the moment they met Mummy, she was warmly embraced as a daughter of the family."

Freda might have had her own reasons to be nervous about what she was walking into. It was well known that in India, brides, including Western ones, are given an extremely hard time, especially by the mother-in-law, who frequently relegates them to the status of servant. Beatings, and worse, are not uncommon. The Bedis, however, were not typical. They were broad-minded, cultured, individualistic, and unconventional to an unusual degree. Freda slipped into her new Indian life with consummate ease.

"The village where BPL's father's home is located is a lovely place on the wide Punjabi plains surrounded by grain fields, and the Himalayas, covered with snow, stretch in an unbroken line only fifty miles away. To see them in the melting heat of a summer day, suspended as it were in a haze of hot air, is unforgettable," she wrote to her friend Olive. "Strangely, I am happier here, despite all the hardness of life from the point of view of Western amenities. The more I see of India, the more I realize I was not built to live in the West. The kind of happiness I feel in an Indian bazaar I never felt in an English street. I am picking up Urdu and Punjabi by degrees and will be thrilled when I am fluent in them."

Initially they moved into a grand house in the Solon Hills belonging to BPL's brother, Trilochan Das (TD Bedi), a session judge, and his modern, English-educated Indian wife. "It's far too anglicized," complained Freda. Almost immediately they joined both the Socialist and Communist parties. Freda took on the extra work of organizing the All India Civil Liberties Union of the Punjab. BPL happily set to work organizing demonstrations, using his brother's car to go from meeting to meeting. TD, as a member of the elite Indian Civil Service, was theoretically on the opposite side of the fence from his brother, but like BPL, he was an independent-minded character.

"Secretly, he was a sympathizer. He refused to welcome the governor general at the airport on the legal grounds that the judiciary was separate from the executive and therefore he was not obliged to turn up. Like my father, he was a rebel—he was suspended several times for wearing Indian clothes into court," said Kabir.

Once Ranga was acclimatized, they swiftly moved to a beautiful bungalow in Lahore, the capital of the Punjab. However, the strength of their principles was challenged in one particularly stark incident, recorded by BPL toward the end of his life.

"We were living a salubrious existence with servants and all the luxuries life could offer. One day some comrades from the country came to visit. It was a very hot summer day, and because they were rough-looking, simple folk, the servants told them, 'Sahib and Memsahib are sleeping. You must stay outside in the garden.' They would not let them enter our house. When we woke, we were shocked at what happened and unanimously decided that very day to give up that way of living. We turned our back on the bungalow, gave away our furniture, and donated many thousands of books that we had brought over from our Oxford days to the Lahore Library."

It was a radical, some would say heroic, stance, but as Freda pointed out, it was underscored by the very practical reality that rent on the bungalow was high and their incomes were abysmally low. Poverty was to stalk them all their married life, as they put principles above financial security.

Through his brother's connections, BPL was offered a job as a professor of Economics at Khalsa College in Amritsar, place of the Golden Temple, and the spiritual home of the Sikhs, but he turned it down on the grounds that the college depended on government funds. To take it would mean giving up his fight for independence. He was becoming increasingly known for stirring up the people to revolution. Nobody dared give him work for fear of retribution from the authorities.

"Life is one long work with rather less than reward in the way of money, but that is inevitable if you are living in an imperialist country and have the temerity to fight the government. The vast majority of all paying jobs are in government, or involve toadying to the government, which neither of us are prepared to do," said Freda. "Spiritually one lives on a precipice here. Both BPL and I are determined that our fight for Indian independence will be the one and only aim of our lives. There is no good or satisfaction in amassing money and possessions, even if I wanted to, when people with any independent political opinions are liable at any minute to be either imprisoned or have their goods confiscated. So we live in a happy-go-lucky fashion and thoroughly enjoy ourselves."

BPL turned to freelance journalism, editing a sports magazine and then founding *Monday Morning*, an outspoken newspaper carrying articles on injustice wherever he and Freda found it. Together they launched a national quarterly journal, *Contemporary India*, which ran articles on current ideas in politics, economics, and philosophy as well as short stories by interesting new writers. Their income was sparse and sporadic.

From this time on, Freda took on the added responsibility of becoming the main breadwinner for the family, a function she fulfilled the entire time she was with BPL. Her workload was always tremendous, as she managed the many tentacles of her career and political calling, along with her home life and motherhood. She wrote book reviews, was a contributor to All India Radio, and became a consultant on a woman's magazine, *Modern Girl*.

She loved journalism. It fulfilled two primary functions—getting her message across (in this case, educating young Indian women about modern ideas) and her deep-seated desire to champion the female sex in general. Inspired by the suffragette movement and Marxism (which was against the exploitation of anybody), Freda was in the vanguard of the feminist movement, long before the term even existed.

In between times, Freda also published *Rhymes for Ranga*, a children's book with Indian themes, which also incorporated subtle political propaganda about the nobility of the peasant and about Gandhi and won a national prize for children's verse.

"Writing gives me and a lot of other people joy. It's amazing that forty years on, some of the articles I wrote are still remembered," she said.

To obtain extra cash, she took a job as the head of the English department at the Fateh Chand College, the first nationalist school for women. She found the work repetitive and boring. "I always hated teaching and still do, but I am glad to do it, because I get in contact with the girls and manage to make them a bit more radical. I hope it bears fruit in the future," she said.

The hours were long and the pay was low, but Freda was a successful teacher in spite of her reservations. Her students grew from twenty-six to six hundred. "There was an insatiable thirst for education among the girls. Their families realized that unless they educated their daughters, their boys would continue to get married abroad and bring home foreign wives," said Freda pragmatically.

To solve the problem of finding somewhere to live, they came up with the novel idea of moving to the newly developed Model Town, on the outskirts of Lahore, designed by Dewan Khem Chand on the ideals of sound ecology and the virtues of community living. As they could not afford one of the houses, they took an acre of land behind the residences (freely given by the landlord, a sympathizer) and proceeded to build a complex of straw-and-mud huts. They moved in together with Bhabooji and three-year-old Barrinder, an orphan of a near-relative. It was basic, back-to-nature living—the simple life advocated by Gandhi. Freda was in heaven.

"Under the trees we built reed huts with thatched roofs and plastered-mud floors, which were extremely beautiful. And we didn't have to pay rent. Our living accommodation consisted of one big hut comprising a dining room, sitting room, and bedroom combined. There was another hut where Bhabooji and the children slept, and a kitchen hut presided over by our great cook, Gut Singh, who stayed with us for about fifteen years. All around us were mustard fields. A stream ran through our land, and we had a buffalo that provided us with milk and freshly churned butter. We cultivated vegetables and I grew a rose garden. Looking back, it had a certain magical, paradisiacal quality, which our visitors never failed to notice."

Ranga, now eighty and living in Bangalore with his artist wife Umi, happily recalls his days in the Hut System. "It was a gorgeous life. I used to run around barefoot, playing with paper boats in the stream and swinging from an eighteen-foot tree, which afforded a huge pendulum arc. Of course, there was no electricity—I can still hear the hiss of the kerosene Ditmar lamps. I had all the pets in the world. There was a pony, which I used to ride for hours every day, two wonderful shepherd dogs called Pug and Smug, which grew so big they presented a massive fighting team against any marauding animals. Later came Rufus, the Great Dane—Papa only liked big dogs. Mummy loved animals too, but feeding them . . . She held the purse strings!

"We had rabbits, guinea pigs, and of course chickens, to satisfy Papa's craving for fresh eggs. The buffalo was my source of milk. Bhabooji would get me up at five in the morning to milk the buffalo and squirt the warm, slightly salty milk directly into my mouth. I was perfectly fine with that. It was getting up at five a.m. that was the pain! Nearby was one of the biggest bungalows with a boy who had a room just for his toys, but even though my life was rustic, I never felt deprived."

Freda became pregnant again and their second son, Tilak Zaheer, was born on November 28, 1935, when Ranga was eighteen months old. Both parents were delighted.

"Tilak was one of the most famous Indian nationalists, and so with Zaheer as his second name he should be a pretty good revolutionary. He is a very serious young man, quite different from Ranga, who has smiled almost since birth," Freda wrote to Olive.

The surroundings may have been utopian, but all was not well in the Hut System. Ranga did not get any real schooling, due to lack of funds, and he contracted typhoid from contaminated hand-pumped water. A doctor strongly advised Freda not to keep the children under such conditions, but as was her wont, she had set her goals and was single-mindedly moving toward them.

The worst happened. Baby Tilak died of dysentery during an epidemic that was sweeping the Punjab. He was just a few months old. Compounding the tragedy, at the time of his death Freda was away campaigning for independence in the countryside, leaving Tilak in the hands of his doting grandmother. On the surface she put a remarkably stoic face on it.

"You must have heard about Tilak," she wrote to Olive. "It was a big shock, but then I am philosophical about these things. I see too much of life not to believe that such troubles are 'all in a day's work,' and that I must leave it. The best consolation is that Ranga is a healthy, high-spirited child, and a joy to us all."

Beneath Freda's most unusual detachment, however, lay a real sense of guilt, as Ranga testified: "Mummy never forgave herself for Tilak's death, because she was not there to look after him. She vowed then not to have another child until Independence was achieved." It was a heavy price to pay in the two-way pull she felt between her deep-seated need to care for "the people" and the equally deep need to care for her own children.

What The Huts lacked in the way of modern conveniences and hygiene was compensated for by the fact that life around Freda and BPL was never dull. The Bedis had an open home, and a constant stream of fascinating visitors were always dropping by and staying, encouraged by the "come on in, sit down, and have a meal" welcome. The majority were the leading left-wingers of the time— artists, poets, and politicians, including Gyani Zail Singh (the first Punjabi to become president of India), I. K. Gujral (thirteenth prime minister of India), Hafeez Jullandhri (poet and composer of the Pakistani national anthem), and Balraj Sahri (the noted film and stage actor). And not least was the mighty Sheikh Abdullah, self-styled "Lion of Kashmir," three times president, who was later to play such a prominent role in their destiny.

"Our home became a center for so many seekers of the truth," said Freda. But life was becoming increasingly tense, both outside and inside The Huts, as the push for a free India gathered pace. And BPL and Freda were thrust into the very forefront.

Circa 1900. The tiny watchmakers shop on Monk Street, Derby, England where Freda Houlston was born. Pictured are her grandfather and father. "As attractive as the Old Curiosity Shop." (Courtesy Pauline Watson.)

Circa 1910. Freda's father, Frank Houlston, who was killed in battle a few weeks before the end of World War I. "His death overshadowed my entire childhood." (Courtesy Pauline Watson.)

The dates listed here are approximate.

1919. Young Freda, always a bookworm, with her mother Nellie, an accomplished dress-maker, and her brother John, whom Freda adored. (Bedi family archives.)

1932. Freda with Baba Phyare Lal Bedi (BPL), the sixteenth direct descendant of Guru Nanak, founder of the Sikh religion, whom she met and married at Oxford, amid much scandal. "You will have to spend our marriage waiting outside jail walls," he told her. (Bedi family archives.)

1932. The young, in-love Freda in heady, Oxford days. Taken by her fiancé BPL. (Bedi family archives.)

1935. Freda as a new bride in India wearing the wedding gift of a sari. She would never wear Western clothes again. (Bedi family archives.)

1935. Freda in Lahore, Pakistan, a week before second son, Tilak, was born. He died a few months old, while Freda was away campaigning for Indian independence. (Bedi family archives.)

1935. Freda dressed completely in khadi, the homespun cloth of devoted Gandhi followers. She was imprisoned for his cause. (Bedi family archives.)

5

Freedom Fighter

HER HOME and working life established, Freda threw herself wholeheartedly into her mission to free India from imperialism and to bring justice and equality to the poor and downtrodden. She traveled all over the Punjab by foot, often taking Ranga with her, going from village to village, absorbing the land and its people, raising their consciousness about the struggle for freedom. She stayed in their huts, ate their food, learned their songs, and heard their problems. Now, rather than being confined to merely looking in and talking as she had as an Oxford undergraduate, she was in a position to act.

This intimacy heightened her love of India and whetted her revolutionary zeal. "India is in a very bad way and constitutions, for all the fuss made over them, are not going to help at all. It will need something more radical. When you get into the homes of the peasants—unbelievable poverty! They live on three paisa per day—one penny, at a liberal estimate—everything inclusive. They are just ground down by starvation and the moneylender," she wrote to Olive. Later, she added, "India has harrowed me with her festering poverty, her dirt, and her despair, and I have become a unit of the ragged army that fights against it."

Freda's compassion and admiration for the peasants never wavered. In her eyes they were noble souls, living a truer existence, in harmony with the soil and the rhythms of the seasons, unsullied by materialism. "Modern people would probably put security at the top of the list of what makes them happy, but the peasant is humbler and simpler in the face of the inevitable insecurities of nature and of life. The villagers, the 'illiterates' of India, have got that genius of simple people; they judge not from words but from the heart, from feelings, from gestures, from instinct. It is we who have been blunted by words, not they who are dull."

Again her affinity with women—especially mothers—was strong. "Many times I have been confronted with a village woman and her child and she has given one look at me and my little boy, and we have been friends from that minute. There is something in the understanding of a woman and a woman, of a mother and a mother, which is far beyond language or skin. It is a feeling often 'too deep for tears,' born of common hopes, and prayers, and sufferings."

Her agenda was twofold: to urge "the warrior peasants of the Punjab" to agitate for land reform and fairer land revenues, and to demand their civil liberties, especially against the heartless Indian police officers, who regularly beat them. She would then bring this terrible treatment to the attention of the authorities.

Word quickly spread of the Englishwoman, dressed in a sari, and her audiences grew from a few stragglers to vast crowds, curious to see and hear this phenomenon for themselves. "When I say that in those days I addressed not just thousands but hundreds of thousands of villagers, I am not telling an untruth. It became part of my way of life. The Punjab peasant became not only familiar to me but a friend."

A far greater challenge was addressing the students and nationalists in Lahore, but BPL urged her to do it. "He said it was nothing, that I should think of it as if I were addressing the debating society at Oxford. The first time I spoke, I was petrified. There were twenty-four thousand people waiting. And these twenty-four thousand people had very definite opinions about what they should and shouldn't listen to. If they didn't like the speaker, they were well known for beating the ground with shoes and sticks.

"I stood on the platform like a martyr awaiting execution and decided to speak very loudly into the loudspeaker. I can still hear the shock that went through the whole mass of twenty-four thousand heads when this rather slight, Western-looking woman suddenly bellowed at them. I found out I could go on speaking and not be drummed out of existence by sticks and shoes."

Freda had well and truly found her voice—an unusual thing for any woman of any era. She was extremely accomplished in her native tongue and loved words, but to give a speech in Hindi (albeit with a British accent) was a remarkable accomplishment. The audience was rightly mesmerized by this woman of the Raj and the wife of one of the biggest landowners of the Punjab, who was urging them on to rebellion. Decades later, people could still recall the power of her oratory. After her inaugural speech there was thunderous applause and cries of, "We want freedom."

Her speeches especially resonated with the women, who took courage from Freda's own example. Freda records how the women of Srinagar ran out in the streets, rattled stones, and frightened the soldiers' horses. "The women became the heroines. Village women would take a club on their shoulder and stride at the head of the village 'armies.' There was nothing dynamic or fiery in their timid faces. But I knew inside me this was woman's shell. When the time came, these women would be on the streets again, never faltering, throwing their powerhouse of energy into another great movement of the people. Women put their proverbial patience to many uses. They know how to wait."

Inevitably, the authorities reacted. Everyone in The Huts lived in a constant state of tension and anxiety. The Huts were constantly threatened with demolition; Freda and BPL (and those who associated with them) were under constant surveillance and were frequently harassed by the police.

"Being a socialist in India is no joke. We all of us live on the edge of jail, and however careful you are, nothing much can be done if you do get arrested, since legal rights are rather pre-Cromwell. It is very difficult to present a picture of these terrifying days," Freda wrote to Olive.

Ranga still remembers the tension that surrounded them all. "Mummy was trailed by plainclothed policemen all the time. In order to get her removed from her job, Fateh Chand College was subjected to all sorts of harassment and sudden inspections, but the school never submitted. It was extremely brave of them, as harboring a political activist was a punishable act. No other college dared employ her, even though a master's degree from Oxford was no mean qualification for a woman in India.

"They even questioned the sweepers to see if she was teaching sedition! Once, when a sweeper was taken down to the police station and manhandled, my mother marched off with me in tow and took the police inspector to task. She then insisted on making a notation in the complaint book. That evening a British police officer visited the college and threatened to arrest her. She wrote to the police hierarchy in Lahore and sent copies to the newspapers. Mummy was absolutely fearless at all times!"

It was the threat of prison, however, that most unnerved Freda. All the A-list agitators, including of course Nehru and Gandhi, were constantly being hauled before judges and jailed. BPL was no exception. He was first arrested in 1937 for some provocative speech at an outdoor meeting, and Freda soon became reconciled to the pattern. It was part of the deal they had signed up for, and what they actually wanted in order to promote their cause. As he had warned as part of his marriage proposal, Freda spent a lot of time visiting him behind bars. Once again she was stoic.

"It is not unduly oppressive and often there are some enlightened Indian officers in charge who are nationalists at heart, and so don't give the prisoners a hard time. Of course, imprisonment is imprisonment, and it's a suffering not be allowed to go out and lead a normal life. But BPL is cheery and philosophical, and usually has one or two good friends in jail with him. My mother-in-law, because of her age and generation, suffers even more than I do about this. We are great friends, and her loving presence makes a great difference."

By 1939, the revolution was heating up, and under Bose's influence, freedom fighters were favoring violence as the means to achieve their goal. This was too much for Freda, who promptly turned her attention totally to Gandhi and his peaceful approach of civil disobedience. BPL, however, jumped right in with added fervor and was promptly arrested for dangerous political activity and sentenced to four years in Deoli Prison (infamous for coining the term *doolally*, signifying "crazy").

Deoli was grim, situated in the middle of the Rajasthan desert, miles from anywhere, and enclosed within three layers of barbed wire and numerous watchtowers. An escapee would have to walk days before reaching the nearest village.

It was the longest sentence BPL had been given and the hardest for Freda to bear, not only because she was left alone without moral and physical support from her husband but also because she rightly knew that BPL would continue to agitate behind bars. She lived in a constant state of worry and fear for him.

Now unable to live independently in The Huts because it was too dangerous, she got permission to move into one of Fateh Chand College's hostels, taking Ranga with her. Children were not allowed into the hostels, but Freda was popular with students and staff alike, having won their admiration and respect. Again, the college bravely agreed. With plenty of staff only too happy to look after (and spoil) Ranga, Freda was free to continue her full teaching program and carry on with her own revolution.

Wracked with anxiety about BPL in Deoli, Freda constantly badgered the prison authorities for the right to visit him. After much string pulling from two barrister friends practicing in the Punjab High Court, Freda finally got a permit for a "family" visit. She took Ranga with her. It turned into a saga of high comic drama.

Ranga recalled, "Mummy and I set off in the blistering heat traveling by train, third class, as she always insisted. It took days, with us staying at small wayside hotels, eating at bus stops and having to report to various police stations along the way. All the time Mummy was harassed so that she would abandon the trip. Finally we were put down beside a dirt track and, after an hour's walk, arrived at Deoli Detention Camp, which was run by the army, not the police. They had no information regarding our visit and were visibly put out by the sight of Mummy in Indian clothes, the British wife of a dangerous political criminal.

"After a short while we were escorted to the commandant, a strapping British colonel whose discomfiture was even greater than that of his juniors. He said he could not allow the visit without confirmation from headquarters. Furthermore, he continued, providing accommodation for a difficult prisoner's wife and child or acquiring transport to the nearest town was out of the question. He didn't know what to do with us. We could see he was rattled, and confused! At sundown he relented and conceded that we could stay in the officers' suite and would be able to meet Papa the next morning, at nine, for one hour. In the end we were given the VIP treatment, including an invitation to dine in the officers' mess hall. Mummy politely declined.

"Mummy was up at first light, and after breakfast (served in our rooms) we were escorted back to the commandant. The atmosphere was tense. The colonel told us there had been an 'incident.' The political prisoners had gone on hunger strike and had had to be force-fed—with the exception of Mr. Bedi, who had aggressively resisted. They had been protesting against prison conditions, alleging it was being run like a concentration camp, with the inmates being denied the rights of political detainees.

"News of our visit had spread, and another attempt to force-feed BPL had been made at six o'clock that morning. Apparently eight people had gone to Papa's room and found him to be calm and generally cooperative. They put together the feeding apparatus, with no protest from Papa. As the medical officer bent over him, Papa sprang into action. He kicked the attendant in the groin, carried him to the door, and threw him off the veranda, causing him to dislocate his shoulder. Two other guards were floored, and the others backed off.

"Mummy remained very calm. 'Didn't you know he holds the All India hammer-throwing record?' she asked. Knowing we were there, Papa said he would eat voluntarily, but only if he could see us.' Of the incident BPL remarked, 'The battle lasted only two minutes, my honor was sustained.'"

The story became apocryphal among the Bedis.

Freda and Ranga finally found BPL the sole occupant of a ten-foot-square room, the last one in a long row in a barrack-like building. There was a mattress on the floor, no furniture or curtain at the window. The books they had brought him were confiscated. The meeting was warm but abysmally short. When they emerged, one of the escorting officers commented, "Mrs. Bedi, your husband is a very strong man." Freda, polite as always and willing to connect with everyone, struck up conversation and was amazed to discover he was from Derbyshire.

After they left, BPL's hunger strike continued for twenty-five days, during which time he received several beatings, which left permanent damage to his spine. He always walked with a cane after that.

The visit marked a turning point in Freda's life. Her marriage was founded on the vow to unite with BPL in his fight for Indian independence, whatever it took. She now decided to join him in jail. Having discussed the matter over with him in Deoli, she applied to become one of Gandhi's handpicked satyagrahis, the select band of protestors who were willing to sacrifice everything, including their lives, to free India from colonial rule. It was the radical move, she told Olive, that was needed to get the job done and give the oppressed a voice. Freda was determined to live out her beliefs to the full, even if it meant leaving Ranga without both parents.

Conceived when Gandhi was working as a lawyer in South Africa, the Satyagraha movement was defined as the Force Born of Truth, Love, and Nonviolence. As his independence movement gathered increasing support, Gandhi rightly judged that a handpicked band of highly committed, disciplined individuals, his satyagrahis, would have a greater impact on public and official opinion than would mob unrest. Furthermore he would run less risk of losing control of them in the heat of the action. Freda explained, "The idea was that only the few would go to jail to protest for the many."

It was a momentous decision, especially in light of the fact that they had already lost one child in the name of their political activities. Torn between compassion for the many and the care of her child, Freda chose the bigger picture. She reasoned that the many, suffering as they were under exploitation and poverty, had no one to champion them, whereas Ranga was surrounded by doting relatives, especially Bhabooji. In the end, as always, Freda followed the force of her convictions.

"I didn't want to make things worse on the domestic side, but on the other hand I felt I should back up the nationalist movement in whatever humble way I could, even if it meant suffering for some months in prison. I also wanted to support BPL and share what he was going through," she reasoned.

Freda began to prepare. She arranged for BPL's brother, the judge, to support her family financially while she was behind bars, and she also carefully explained to Ranga what she was going to do and why.

"Mummy swore me to secrecy. I couldn't talk about it to anyone! I was really scared. I had this persistent raw feeling in the pit of my stomach. I remember one incident when Mummy took us to have our anti–cholera-and-typhoid injections and the doctor said, 'Freda, it's very wise to have these shots before offering Satyagraha,' and the raw feeling intensified," Ranga recalled.

Over the next few months she took her son back for extended visits to the family land at Dera Baba Nanak, where his paternal grandmother and her extended family were living, to acclimatize him to the impending separation. It was a clever move.

"I loved it at Bhabooji's. I was given an endless supply of sweets, was allowed to stay up and sleep in late, and was given a pair of quails, and a parrot, and was made the sole egg collector. On my return to Fateh Chand College I could hardly wait for Mummy to go through with her plans."

Freda waited some time to be chosen, but she was finally accepted by Gandhi as his fifty-seventh satyagrahi—the first British woman to be admitted to his elite band. Instructions came: On no account was she to retaliate or resist if she were arrested or beaten. The main thrust of her protest, like that of all satyagrahis, was to speak out against "the crime" of involving India in Britain's participation in World War II without first consulting the legislative assembly. Gandhi argued that to fight another nation's war without personal choice was unacceptable. (Ironically, Freda seemed not to notice that Britain's war was against fascism, the very thing that she, too, declared she loathed.)

She duly wrote to the district magistrate informing him that she intended to break the law by holding a mass rally during which she would urge the people not to support the military effort until India became a democracy and they could choose for themselves. But for all her outer composure, when the day came, Freda admitted she was scared.

"Suddenly I felt alone, agonizingly alone. I could have wept for my sheer aloneness. I wanted to talk to BPL, to have his cheery voice near me," she said. "I suppose in all crises of our life we get that feeling of isolation as though we are treading a path into the future all alone, for all the love that surrounds us—when we first leave home, when we marry, when we have a choice to make at some crossroads of our life. Perhaps we feel like that when we are on the brink of death. And on the borders of that aloneness, there comes another feeling, of being given the strength to carry on, of not being alone anymore."

Freda was buoyed up by the breadth of her vision, and the revolution she hoped she would ignite: "That spark will go on burning until it ignites a greater fire than the one from which it sprang. And you are the spark of a greater fire, although you barely know it," she said.

February 21, 1941, was the day Freda chose to make her biggest protest yet. However, in the hours beforehand, a comic cat-and-mouse game with the police was played out.

"First a local inspector arrived to inquire about her plans and to inform her she was being put under twenty-four-hour surveillance," says Ranga. "Then several police surrounded the house and compound. Mummy's response was to send tea and snacks out to them every few hours. In the meantime huge crowds were gathering, and the villagers, undeterred by the police presence, erected a small stage from which she could address the rally. The police tried to pull it down, but they could not get close enough. Their plan was to arrest her before she reached the stage.

"At four a.m., when it was still dark, the police burst into the house, but Mummy was nowhere to be found. They searched the surrounding farmhouses, but to no avail, so they started a rumor that she had already been arrested in the hope that the multitude would disperse. By now some forty thousand people had arrived by train, bullock cart, or on foot to witness an Englishwoman offering Satyagraha, and there was something of a carnival atmosphere.

"Mummy suddenly appeared, as if from nowhere. She had been hiding under the stage. It was the most dramatic event of my early life. Mummy was utterly calm, but I was shaking. She told the crowd that any form of violence or resistance to her arrest would defeat the cause and would deeply disappoint her, leading her to regard it as a failure of her mission. She went on to say she had chosen Dera because it was the home of Baba Nanak and the Bedi clan. Mummy then came over to me and gave me a big hug."

Freda recounted, "A local policeman with a beard came forward politely. 'Regretting it is my duty, but I must arrest you,' he said. To his right was the English police inspector from Amritsar, who was there because they did not know how an Englishwoman might react when she was arrested. He was surprisingly small, in an unwieldy toupee and had a walrus mustache. He looked like Old Bill. I wanted to laugh, and the corners of my mouth twitched. 'I am quite ready. Take me along with you,' I said."

It took Freda and the policemen at least thirty minutes to get through the throng, who were all shouting, "Freedom for India! Long live Gandhiji! Long live Comrade Bedi! Release the Detainees!" and were throwing garlands over the awaiting car. "Garlands are not allowed," said Old Bill. The villagers peered wonderingly into the car as it sped Freda away.

At the police station the comedy continued. Following procedure, Old Bill asked her nationality. "English." Where was she born? "Derby." What color would she say her eyes were? "You might call them blue-gray." She was taken swiftly on to the courtroom. The trial took fifteen minutes, with an embarrassed, red-faced young judge, fresh out of England, admitting to her, "I find this as embarrassing as you do."

Freda looked directly into his eyes and replied, "Don't worry, I don't find it unpleasant at all. Treat me as an Indian woman and I will be quite content."

After fumbling in his Defense of India rules book the judge

handed her the sentence: six months' rigorous imprisonment in Lahore female jail.

"Surely you mean Lahore Women's Jail," Freda replied archly, offended by his grammar.

The sentence was exceptionally harsh—no other satyagrahi was given as much. Freda reacted with customary composure, and with no anger or malice. There was even kindness. 'Maybe it was because they wanted to make an example out of me, because I was English and the first Western woman to offer Satyagraha. Or maybe it was the ignorance of the young civil servant presiding at the trial. He gave the sentence regretfully and with many apologies. He was a decent sort of man," she said.

Freda was just thirty years old when she went to jail. She had come a long way from the little watchmaker's shop in Derby. In those years she had become a trailblazer, defying expectations and convention by marrying a Sikh, living in a left-wing commune, and raising literally thousands of people to insurrection by the power of her oratory—all in the name of humanity and justice.

6

Prisoner

CONVICT NO. 3613 started her prison sentence on a suitably rebellious note by refusing to hand over her wedding ring, which was classified as jewelry. It had not left her finger since the day she married BPL, and she was not prepared to part with it now. Drawing herself up to her full height and putting on her most English accent, she quoted her rights as a Class A political prisoner, which did not state that "jewelry" had to be relinquished. She won.

Next step was getting what was called her "history ticket": weight, 132 pounds; height, five feet six and a half inches; occupation, professor of English; crime, political; sentence, six months' "rigorous imprisonment." She was then marched through a barred outer gate and inner iron door that reminded her of entering a safe, and began her incarceration.

It was not the dank, rat-infested hellhole one might imagine. Her cell was a room, which she shared with other satyagrahis—all self-sacrificing Indian women, who warmly welcomed the infamous white woman into their midst. Her time as a prisoner was recorded in a diary—later published in a book she wrote, *Behind Mud Walls*.

"My cell mates are quiet, determined souls, not noisy rebels, the stuff of which Gandhi's little army is made. They are not professional politicians, but widows and married women who have left behind their children, husbands, and households to offer themselves up (for arrest) in the service of their country."

Freda laid out her bedroll on the floor and began her life behind bars. She adapted relatively easily to the regime, which by Western standards was remarkably relaxed. Together the women cooked their own meals on firewood fires with basic rations issued by the prison: cooking fat, sugar, flour, bread, vegetables, milk, tea, and spices. Occasionally their diet was brightened by provisions sent in from family and friends, which they shared. Freda received baskets of fruit and, most incongruously, flowers from admirers and well-wishers. A particular bouquet of nasturtiums, sweet peas, and cornflowers elicited an ecstatic diary entry: "Flowers in jail! What they mean only a prisoner can know."

It was an extraordinarily social environment. Women had their babies with them in jail, and friends sometimes volunteered to be inside simply to keep their loved ones company. When they weren't working, they sang and danced, especially on feast days, beating drums and swirling their skirts. Freda noted that the laxity of rules was excellent for keeping tension at bay and making imprisonment bearable. (It helped that the deputy superintendent had been one of Freda's students.) The guards even turned a blind eye, or ear to the revolutionary songs with their theme of independence.

"It was the go-ahead to revolt—to resist autocracy with every fiber of our being—and fight for the ultimate human values, the freedom of the human spirit," Freda said.

Her "hard labor" was not hauling bricks or smashing rocks but working in the prison garden from 8:00 a.m. until noon, and again from 1:00 to 5:00 p.m. Of all punishments, nothing could have suited nature-loving Freda better. It was a godsend. She set to work tilling the soil, tending the fruit trees and vegetables: marrows, cucumbers, onions, okra, lemons, mangoes, and mulberries. Surrounded by plants and birds, the mystical Freda was often "transported" beyond the prison walls. Her diary records how entranced she was by the early hooting of an owl, the tenderness of a pair of parrots making love, the crows flying purposefully home. And when the garden bloomed, she became positively ecstatic.

"The garden in the early morning is delirious with young leaves, the scent of orange blossom and the crimson roses smelling like heaven. I've never seen so many roses in my life as I have this past fortnight. I put them in earthenware pots and brass bowls and then haven't anything to eat off or cook in."

Freda was always good at putting a positive spin on even the most difficult of situations (and people), however, and a later diary entry when the summer was upon her reveals how much her survival in jail depended on the healing power she found in nature. "Out into the garden when the moon and evening star were together in the sky. It was a soft dark green everywhere after the thunder and rain last night—and it consoled me as it has always done. I can't live without green things. If I hadn't had even this bit of dryish jungle here, I would have dried up myself and become ill," she confessed.

When she wasn't outside, Freda kept busy. She taught English, gave lectures on Marx, and as Gandhi exhorted, she spun cloth. Initially Freda found it soothing, but she spun so enthusiastically that she developed eczema on her hands.

Life behind bars was not all song, dance, and learning. The harsh reality of incarceration soon hit. She missed Ranga terribly and applied for permission to have him to visit. After a long wait, it was granted. The experience was difficult. "Ranga stayed overnight, sleeping with his little arms thrown drowsily around me, creating a night of bitter-sweet intensity, before he was off again, leaving me alone," she said.

From the beginning, Freda was perpetually wracked with anxiety and longing for BPL, who was locked away in his own jail cell, miles away. She missed him deeply and wrote him copious letters and telegrams asking how he was. At first all she received was silence. Every day her diary tells how she pined for him, especially on April 5, his birthday.

"Being physically and mentally cut off from him, I am thrown even more into myself. His jailers and mine can't cut me off from thinking about him; my thoughts burn like a flame so that sometimes we are no longer apart. I try to project my love toward him, to strengthen and protect him," she wrote.

Eventually a telegram arrived: "Happy Beloved, letter following million tons love." It was so sudden she was utterly taken aback. Four days later the letter arrived. Holding it in her hands, Freda felt turned over inside. In true BPL style it blithely informed her that he had acquired a ten-day-old orphaned deer and a goat foster mother! Freda relaxed. With baby animals to care for, she knew her husband was happy.

As the weeks wore on and the heat grew fiercer, life for Freda grew tougher in all respects. In the garden her "hard labor" began to earn its name. With temperatures reaching 115 degrees, the searing heat made her exhausted and demoralized. The water supply for the plants she worked so diligently on dried up, ruining her garden. She saw the earth turn to dust and wizened little lemons drop to the ground. Her nerves, always fragile, were stretched to the breaking point. When her pleas for more water fell on deaf ears, for once, self-contained, polite Freda lost her temper and shouted at the guards. Afterward, she felt ashamed.

Her situation was exacerbated by insomnia. The heat was not only preventing her from sleeping at night, she was unable to nap in the afternoon because of the pigeons clattering about on the roof above her head. "I could have broken all my vows of nonviolence on them," she said. The heat also made the toilets almost unbearable to the dirt-loathing Freda. They were ancient, foul, open to the elements, with only a flapping curtain for privacy. She was faced with the alternative of carrying an umbrella to protect her from the elements, which meant either putting her head in the revolting cloth or pushing aside the curtain and risking being seen. She did her best to block out the smells and sights, but it didn't work. "If I were to give way to what I truly feel, I would be sick every time I go near the place," she said.

News that the inmates of Deoli were threatening yet another hunger strike ratcheted up Freda's tension even further. She confessed she was literally worried sick, and vomited frequently. Knowing there was a heat wave there didn't help. "They have no fans at Deoli. I wish things could be settled without this wringing of the heart," she said.

In jail, Freda's concerns and compassion stretched beyond her husband. In the garden she was mingling with an array of colorful, nonpolitical women prisoners, who were certainly not the peaceful satyagrahis with whom she shared a room. She got to know them all—drug smugglers, gypsies, embezzlers, and murderers. She listened to their stories of abduction and poverty, the latter often due simply to the awful financial calamity of having too many girl babies, and was filled with pity, understanding, and indignation.

"These jail women wring my heart. They may be guilty, but what does that really mean here? Either that they loved another man and ran away with him—a thing that happens hundreds and thousands of times in the West—or that they were the helpless tool of some man's guile. Many women have deliberately chosen jail as being preferable to life with a despotic, exploitative old man. It's tragic that they can do nothing and must suffer like common felons." she said.

She tried to help by sharing with them the "beauties" of socialism and the horrors of fascism, and sometimes she even gave legal advice. "There is a sixteen-year-old girl here whose seventy-year-old husband sent her out onto the streets to beg and for prostitution. He also bit off her ear. When she ran away, he had a case framed against her. I recommended she demand a divorce through lawyers. Anything is better than living with that old satyr."

Her concern and compassion went far beyond the prison's bars, however. She was all too well aware that World War II was escalating in Europe, and this increased her anguish for the suffering she knew was being unleashed. Those others, so far away, she could not help. "I sometimes feel the awful agony of the world like a dark cloud above my head. It is almost unbearable to think of the brutalities and stupidities of man committed upon man," she said. Later this widespread, deep-felt empathy for the pain of others in general and the wish for it to cease would be regarded as a mark of a genuine *bodhisattva*—the heroic Buddhist practitioner fired with altruistic intention to relieve all beings of their sorrows and fundamental ignorance, which prevented them from seeing the true nature of reality and their indwelling magnificent buddha nature.

She was particularly worried about her mother, left behind in England, knowing too well the trauma she'd gone through during World War I with the loss of her husband. A letter from Nellie finally reached her in jail. It contained a ten-shilling note (a belated and very welcome birthday present) and news that Freda's and BPL's imprisonment had made the British newspapers. Freda knew how shocking the reports would have read (along the lines of "British Woman Turns Traitor") and was relieved that Nellie seemed to be not unduly horrified at her maverick daughter's latest scandal:

"It's easier now that I know Mother has taken it so well," she said before continuing on a more defiant note that underlined her unswerving dedication to her beliefs. "Not that I would have altered my course of action, but I hate to cause her pain. I know she is suffering, but there is no panic, and friends have rallied around her. I'm glad, for few must have understood what it was all about. Anti-Fascist though we are, and have been for years, it is hard for the average British citizen who isn't very interested in politics to understand what resistance to imperialism means, what India is really feeling, how severely her self-respect has been wounded, how she is ready and willing to fight oppression and aggression to vindicate her denied nationhood."

By May, Freda began to hear whispers that legal moves were afoot to get her an early release. It was true. A certain Justice Bhide gave an enterprising judgment in the High Court that claimed that sending a letter to a magistrate announcing one's intention to break the law (as Freda had done) did not constitute an offense in itself. In fact, he argued, it was a prevention of a crime! Over the next few days, the news became more certain. On May 23, Freda was informed that she was to be released the very next day, triggering a round of farewell parties from the other inmates, who were sad to see her go.

When the jail doors opened just after noon on May 24, 1941, Freda walked into freedom and a rapturous welcome from a small group of Indian National Congress supporters. A large party had been organized in her honor, where food and speeches were to be offered, but Freda declined. She gave instructions, however, that she was prepared to do whatever Congress wanted of her. If they required her to go back to prison, she would happily agree. Going to prison for her beliefs had filled her with a deep sense of satisfaction, fulfillment, and strength.

She sent telegrams to BPL and her mother telling them of her release and then made her way back to Dera Baba Nanak, the Bedi ancestral home, where she had been arrested.

Her triumphant homecoming is etched vividly in Ranga's memory. "Late one afternoon, a message came from Lahore that Mummy's release was imminent, she would come straight to us in Dera. On a rainy afternoon we could hear sounds of slogans being shouted in the distance. I ran straight through the front gate and through the fields where a bullock cart was approaching. Mummy was crouched under a shawl surrounded by several others all crammed into the cart. A huge sirdar (Sikh) picked me up and put me next to her. She pulled me under her shawl and gave me an enormous, tight hug.

"Mummy greeted Bhabooji with the traditional touching of the feet, and then the nightmare began. Within an hour dozens of relatives, accompanied by others, began to descend. The next morning it got worse—hundreds of bullock carts laden with families and villagers arrived for darshan (blessing). It was decided that another platform should be built outside the gate, where Mummy could sit and bless the people. For two days people filed past—and then on the fourth and final day Mummy was taken around the village on a bullock cart."

To the people, Freda had become more than a political activist, she had been virtually beatified. From then on, Freda became a national heroine, her fame, influence, and power growing stronger every day. This was to become invaluable in the work that lay ahead. Personally, however, she gained no pleasure from the fuss and the fanfare that greeted her when she emerged from jail. Instead she found it utterly exhausting after the confinement of her little world behind bars. She longed for nothing more than to be alone with Ranga, and to have a cold bath.

Freda had served half of her six-month sentence. During that time she had put on two pounds (from sitting still too much), and had improved her spinning from 225 yards with number-14 yarn per hour to 387 yards with number-18 yarn. She also succeeded in having the name changed from the irksome, grammatically incorrect

Lahore Female Jail to Lahore Women's Jail. She had three rupees to her name.

Prison, she concluded, had taught her much, especially about herself. "I discovered I do not mind being restricted to a small place. I used to imagine before I was released that I would long to be again in the wide world beyond the walls. But I don't. Perhaps I am a bit of hermit and I live a good deal inside myself. Whatever the reason, I felt no more irked than if I had been in a small village and unable to go to town (which I never liked much anyway).

"The thing that troubled me most was not being alone. Being continuously surrounded by chattering, singing, laughing women was sheer emotional and mental torture. However nice they were, their presence permeated me too much and I began to lose myself." Her words hinted at the path that was to be her final destiny—the path of a nun.

Shortly after her release, Freda heard rumors that her husband was being moved from Deoli, because the detention camp was being prepared for prisoners of war. It was thought that BPL was going to be transferred to another prison, but much to the family's amazement, he simply walked into Dera Baba Nanak one evening. The same victory parades that had regaled Freda's return were now staged for BPL, but this time the couple stood on the bullock cart side by side.

7

Kashmir

FAR FROM BEING bowed from her time in jail, over the next four years Freda increased her efforts to bring freedom to the Indian subcontinent. She continued giving speeches in towns and villages, championing the exploited, fighting injustice, and working around the clock to earn a living to support the family. Increasingly her attention was drawn to Kashmir, the exquisitely beautiful but politically volatile state in northwest India famed for its snow-capped peaks, verdant pastures, and Dal Lake with its charming houseboats.

The lure was their close friend Sheikh Mohammad Abdullah, president of Kashmir's first political party, the National Muslim Conference, which he founded in 1932. In June 1939 he changed the name to the more secular sounding All Jammu and Kashmir National Conference. The Bedis and Sheikh Abdullah had much in common. Both believed in equal rights for all sections of society regardless of caste, creed, or religion. Both were adamant about overthrowing imperialism, which in Sheikh Abdullah's case took the form of the Raj-appointed maharaja of Jammu and Kashmir, Hari Singh. Self-rule was the mutual goal.

Sheikh Abdullah was a towering figure. He wore long regal robes and called himself "the Lion of Kashmir." Like BPL, he was charismatic, forceful, and extremely determined. He was also a hunted man. The maharaja was after him, and so were the law enforcers of the British Raj. When he was banned from entering Kashmir, he rushed for sanctuary with Freda and BPL in The Huts. With enormous courage they took him in.

Freda, however, went several steps further. In order to get

Sheikh Abdullah's messages to his many thousands of followers, she elected to carry them herself, disguised in a burka. Inevitably she was discovered and given forty-eight hours to get out of Kashmir. Freda announced, "I'm going to do nothing of the kind," and surreptitiously continued carrying messages.

During these years, fighting for Kashmir, Freda's tenacity and courage became legendary. When the police discovered her staying in a hotel owned by a Sheikh Abdullah sympathizer in Srinagar, they stormed it, forcing her eviction. She found refuge with a houseboat owner on Dal Lake, who hid her in the kitchen. The police were hot on her heels; discovering her hiding place, they roughed up the houseboat owner and his family. Freda returned from her mission to find them in tears and beating their chests. Without a moment's hesitation she sprang into action.

"Mummy immediately got into a rowboat that took her to shore, where she climbed into a *tonga* (horse-drawn carriage) to look for the policemen," reports Ranga. "She found them at a tea shop. After asking them why they had molested the family, she took off her shoe and began to hit them. They ran for their lives, nonplussed that a British woman was beating them.

"Mummy was quite expecting to be arrested again, and was ready for it, but the maharaja thought better of it. He didn't want the scandal of incarcerating her with its attendant publicity of what she had done—it made the police look too silly."

On another occasion it was Freda herself who was hurt—and this time she had taken Ranga with her. They were in Srinagar for a riverboat procession down the Jhelum River to celebrate the fact that Sheikh Abdullah had changed the name of his party from Muslim Conference to National Conference, indicating its nonsectarian basis. Sheikh Abdullah was willing to embrace all faiths in his cause. As the boats, with Freda, Ranga, BPL, and all of Sheikh Abdullah's top guns, sailed down the river, they saw the maharaja's people gathering on the banks to protest.

"As the boats passed under the bridges, they hurled stones down on us, including Mummy, who lay on top of me to protect me. Many people got injured, but I was OK. As for Mummy, she just carried on. She was utterly fearless," said Ranga.

This oblivion to danger was exemplified in one vivid event, when Freda took Ranga camping high into the mountains to escape the Punjab's searing summer heat. They reached Pahalgam, a beautiful and remote spot situated at an altitude of 8,990 feet, and pitched their tents.

"It was stunning, and utterly isolated. We were completely alone up there—the nearest habitation was a small store about three miles away. Papa was not with us, and I was really enjoying having Mummy to myself for once. One morning we woke up to find the upper flap of one of the tents had been torn. A bear had come during the night. Rather than pack up and leave immediately, Mummy lit a bonfire every night between the tents, saying that would do the trick. I wasn't scared. Mummy was always calm and unshakable, and that infused me with a sense of stability in spite of the constant dramas going on in her life," said Ranga.

During her treks in the Kashmiri hills, Freda met the renowned British writer Rumer Godden (author of *Black Narcissus* and *The Greengage Summer*, among other highly esteemed literary works), who lived in a charming pink-and-gray cottage called Dove House halfway up the slopes to the orchard where Freda had pitched her tent. With her uncanny knack for drawing the famous, talented, and unconventional into her orbit, the two women became close friends. Freda was delighted.

They had a lot in common. Both women were literary, loved the arts, had children, and were broke. Rumer's husband had abandoned her, leaving her with a mountain of debt that she paid off from the proceeds of her books. Like Freda, she lived in a romantic dwelling built by a poet, with no running water, no electricity or any form of heating—a serious disadvantage in the snowbound Kashmiri winters. Like Freda, she attracted the bizarre and the dangerous. She discovered her cook was a homicidal maniac when her Pekingese puppy died and she and her family suffered horrifying hallucinations: He had been mixing powdered glass, marijuana, and belladonna into the midday meal of rice and dal.

Another illustrious figure who came into Freda's life at this time was Jawaharlal Nehru, who was to become India's first prime minister. He had met Freda in the early thirties at a Congress convention and admired her greatly, especially after her imprisonment. In addition to Indian self-rule, he too was keenly interested in socialism and women's emancipation. Nehru passionately loved Kashmir, his ancestral home, and took every opportunity to go there. At such times Freda would often drop in, and she became close friends with his daughter, Indira, who was just six years younger, and also Oxford educated. The relationship was sealed when Freda and BPL were invited to Indira's wedding to Feroze Gandhi (no relation), in 1942.

Ranga was at the celebration. "I remember it was held in a large house—and Mummy was the only British face there. Afterward we went to have breakfast with Nehru. We all stayed friends for years. Indira's sons, Rajiv and Sanjay, and became our playmates. Many years later Indira attended my wedding to Umi."

For all her political work, her teaching, her family, her marriage, and her writing, it would be wrong to think that Freda had forsaken her spiritual quest. Far from it. If anything, living in India had only heightened her deep yearning for spiritual nourishment and education. She did yoga (even in jail) and read as much spiritual literature as she could, including the Koran, the Bhagavad Gita, and the Bible, searching for the eternal verities that lay beyond dogma. "I am going through the Old Testament again, leaving out the Rules and the begats. The Gita says that all paths lead to Me. That I believe," she said. What she was looking for was a path that she could devote all her attention and energy to. It was still a way off.

She meditated on her own, compelled to find a space of inner stillness, which she claimed was essential to her very sanity. Meditation, in fact became the fuel that drove all her many endeavors. Just as she had as a young girl, she still somehow knew intuitively that the answers she was seeking were ultimately not to be found between the pages of any religious book but through direct personal experience.

"Bringing up my children, carrying on my life as a teacher, writer, and speaker, I would find that without this time of quietness I could not reach into the deepest reaches of my mind, and the full potentiality of the mind could not be released. The questions kept haunting me: What is the meaning of life? Why is it like this? How can we understand? Who is to tell us? We can't get it from books. We can only get it from within. That's what sustained me," she said.

An interesting side effect of Freda's daily meditation practices, she said, was an increase in her clairvoyance: "I got many internal revelations, even visions," she said later in a radio interview in New York. She discovered she could receive messages via dreams, for example. On one occasion Freda was able to reassure an old college friend living in Malaysia during the outbreak of the war that her missing husband was not dead, as she feared, because she had dreamed of her, her two children, and her husband escaping from the Japanese. Sure enough, four years later the husband emerged from the jungle where he had been hiding and was reunited with his family.

By 1943, the war was beginning to turn against Germany, and two years later, in May 1945, peace was finally declared, ending the global onslaught of terror, destruction, and death. Freda began to relax. She could sniff freedom in the air for India too, the goal that she had dedicated her life to since the moment she set foot in India. She and BPL had patiently waited for twelve years to increase their family and produce a sibling for Ranga. Now, she felt, her job was nearing completion and it would be safe for her to have another child. She would have the time and energy to devote to a new baby, unlike with Tilak. Freda promptly became pregnant.

She had another prophetic dream in which she saw a Tibetan figure holding a boy in front of him. He said to her, "Take care of him." However, at this point in her life, she knew no Tibetans—they had yet to pour out of their homeland into exile. The dream was a harbinger of things to come.

On January 16, 1946, Freda gave birth to her second son, whom they named Kabir, after the sixteenth-century much-loved mystic poet and saint who preached peace between Hindus and Muslims, and the oneness of all religions. From the outset, Freda regarded Kabir as a special child and the closest to her of all her children. Sheikh Abdullah sent a congratulatory telegram from Riasi jail, where he was serving one of his many prison sentences. "He will grow up, I am sure, as a very handsome boy and his forehead depicts him to be a great thinker and revolutionary. May he live long and have a happy life."

Kabir fit happily into The Huts commune where he was guarded by Rufus, the Great Dane (his chowkidar, as BPL called him), given milk by Clarabelle the buffalo, and doted on by Ranga.

In 1947, as Independence neared, Freda returned to England to attend a large socialist conference and to see her mother and show her the new child. On August 15, 1947, at the stroke of midnight while she was in England, Indian independence was declared. After all her work and sacrifice, ironically Freda had missed it. Jawaharlal Nehru, India's leading statesman and its first prime minister, made one of the most eloquent speeches in history. He said, "Long years ago we made a tryst with destiny. And now the time comes when we shall redeem our pledge, not wholly or in full measure, but substantially. At the stroke of the midnight hour, while the world sleeps, India will awake to life and freedom."

She would have dearly loved to be there celebrating with her husband and all her friends, but BPL had warned her to stay away. Already the tension between Hindus and Muslims was mounting, and BPL knew the bloodshed that was about to occur. He had written her an urgent letter saying, "Don't come back to Lahore at this time, whatever you do."

He was right. At the same time an independent, free India was born, a brand-new country, the Muslim state of Pakistan was also created, out of what had formerly been known as the Punjab.

It should have been a moment of great joy and celebration. Instead India awoke to a bloodbath. Rather than being united under the banner of freedom, the subcontinent was abruptly split apart on the basis of religion. A massive cross-migration had begun, with thousands of Muslims fleeing India to get to Pakistan, and Hindus and Sikhs going in the opposite direction to India. The Punjab bore the brunt of it. Lahore, the capital (and Freda's and the Bedis' home) found itself on the Pakistani side of the border, while Amritsar (the Sikhs' holiest place) was a few miles into India.

While Nehru was giving his speech, Lahore was ablaze, with riots in the streets as gangs of Sikhs and Muslims clashed. By

August 15, Lahore was on fire. Over the following days it only got worse. Muslims, Sikhs, and Hindus all engaged in sprees of slaughter, rape, and carnage. Trainloads of refugees that had been hijacked en route arrived at stations filled with dead bodies. Women were stripped naked, paraded through streets, raped, and tattooed with their rapists' names. Corpses piled up on street corners. Villagers were hacked to pieces, babies were burned. Temples were razed to the ground. There was a total collapse of public order, as police stood by or joined in, according to their religious affiliations. The stench of death and burning filled the air. It was estimated that more than half a million people were killed and more than a million made homeless.

For Freda it was physically, emotionally, ethically, and spiritually devastating. "I never felt there was any difference between Hindus and Muslims," she said. "We lived in a society that respected people of all religions, castes, and creeds. But when the Punjab was broken up, we had the traumatic experience of seeing rifts and fissures, yawning like gulfs, between people suddenly divided against themselves. It was shocking and terrible for us—we who had lived in an atmosphere of harmony."

According to Kabir, the ever-confident BPL faced the crisis head-on. "Father was in Lahore, right on the border. He helped people going both ways! He pretended to be whoever might be useful in the moment—he could speak all languages—and would talk his way out of every situation each time he was confronted."

One of the greatest tragedies of India's independence was that the Sikhs lost their homeland, an irony not lost on the Bedis, who had put their hearts and souls into the battle. They could no longer stay in Lahore, which the *Times of India* now described as "a city of the dead." Nehru had gone there himself to plead for peace, to no avail, and declared himself "sick with horror" at the sight of thousands, mostly Sikhs and Hindus, lying dead following the frenzy of killing.

Packing their meager belongings, Freda, BPL, Ranga, and baby Kabir moved to Kashmir, the beautiful land north of the Punjab. The idealistic, romantic, basic, and communal life in The Huts was over. A new era was beginning.

8

Aftermath

IN THE LAST few weeks of 1947, the Bedis moved into a fine gabled house on the edge of Dal Lake that was equipped with comforts and conveniences unheard of in The Huts. They had been drawn not by the landscape but by their great friend Sheikh Abdullah, who was now prime minister of the cojoined State of Jammu and Kashmir. He was promising everything they believed in—religious harmony between Muslims, Sikhs, Hindus, Christians, and Harijans (the Untouchables); female emancipation; and land reform. They were delighted to support him. In Freda's eyes, Sheik Abdullah was virtually a saint.

"He is a Moses-like figure who has, along with his party, led the Kashmiris out of the virtual slavery of the maharaja's kingly rule to responsible government, and given a new self-respect to these gifted people. To this country, whose beauty is tragically silhouetted against the great, unchanging poverty of its peasants and working classes, he and his government have brought fresh faith and a new approach," she said.

Freda's secret ambitions went even higher, however. With her soft guiding hand, she hoped that Kashmir and its co-state, Jammu, would become the blueprint for the rest of the new India to emulate. It was political ideology of the highest order, an audacious, possibly arrogant dream, driven not by the greed for political power but by an altruistic ideal to create that better, fairer, happier world that she had been chasing since Oxford.

Right now, her hero and his state were in deep trouble. Tens of thousands of tribal warriors were pouring over the northwestern frontier from Pakistan, hell-bent on taking Srinagar, with its airport, and making it their own. These were the Pathans, the famous fiercest Islamic fighting force in the world, who were raping, pillaging, and hacking to death every infidel they could find in revenge for the massacres carried out on their Muslim brothers in the border areas. They were stopped at Baramulla, a town a few miles upstream from Srinagar, but not before the town had been reduced to ashes, and its inhabitants—including the Irish nuns at the Baramulla Convent and a priest and nurses in the Baramulla Hospital— had been butchered.

Freda and BPL nobly rushed to the rescue. "We decided we could be most useful in Kashmir and that where our friends were in danger, we should add our might to the struggle, which we had in effect been a part of for so many years," Freda said. "It had never been our fate since our marriage in 1934, to live a particularly safe life in the political conditions then obtaining in India, and we had hoped that with the dawn of Independence we should have a chance to settle down to solid, constructive work to build up a free India, with so many millions of our fellow countrymen and women. But there was a stretch of danger and difficulty still to be crossed."

The air was thick with tension. Kashmir balanced precariously on the brink as it struggled to decide where it was going to place itself—whether it would join with the Muslims in the newly formed Pakistan or accede to union with India. The tug-of-war was fraught, passionate, and vicious.

Freda admitted in a letter to Olive how grim it was. "It has been a new world, both harrowing and inspiring. As you can imagine, it was an electric situation. The tribal raiders (helped by copious drafts of Pakistani petrol, modern firearms, and a hard core of Pakistani officers and men) had been stopped within a few hundred yards of Srinagar by the first Indian troops, who'd been flown in in the nick of time. We more or less camped out in our new house in Srinagar along with the family Great Dane, who has the color and appearance of a young lion."

Freda jumped right in to start helping restore order to the chaotic, dangerous situation

"The first thing Mummy did when we got to Kashmir was to get a group together and go to the church to clean it up. I was with her. Statues had been defaced and were lying smashed. She got down on her hands and knees to clean the blood off the floor and walls. The marauders had used machetes—blood was everywhere. The horror of it only urged her on," recalled Ranga, who was fourteen years old at the time.

The second thing Freda did was to rush to the aid of the multitude of refugees arriving daily from the occupied territories in a constant stream of misery. "Refugees were pouring into Srinagar from all the enemy-occupied areas and battle fronts, a few with some meager possessions, the majority with nothing more than what they stood up in, and these mostly cotton summer clothes utterly inadequate in face of the approaching winter. Their number in Srinagar city alone reached seventeen thousand, no small number to house, feed, and clothe throughout that long, bleak winter, the worst, as luck would have it, for forty years. It snowed for three solid months—we were completely cut off by snow on the one remaining pass, and no plane could land."

Freda focused on the women and children, setting up twenty-three milk-and-relief centers and recruiting a band of Kashmiri girls to help her. "We all acted as older sisters to the thousands of children and women suffering not only physical hardships in the desperate cold but often mental torture when relations and children had been killed, abducted, or lost in the miserable trek to safety," she said. "It was exhausting work—there wasn't time to breathe."

Ranga witnessed what his mother went through. "It was a nightmare. Utter chaos. Everything had shut down, including the schools. Mummy worked around the clock, leaving at seven a.m. and coming home around ten p.m. She was organizing it all—the camps, the food, the medical supplies, the tents. Selfless volunteers were coming in from everywhere, and Mummy organized them too. She was absolutely hands-on."

Freda wasn't the only eminent Englishwoman helping the refugees. Edwina Mountbatten, wife of the last viceroy of India, tirelessly worked with the displaced and wounded after Independence, and she, too, appeared by Freda's side. She declared herself deeply shocked by what she saw in Srinagar but was full of admiration at the sight of the women engaged in the relief effort. "It is always true that good comes out of evil and that there is no doubt that this crisis has brought out women to play their full part in their country's affairs, which would otherwise have taken years of evolution to achieve," she wrote in a letter to Sheikh Abdullah.

Edwina Mountbatten and Freda Bedi were clearly united in their outlook and mission. Edwina's next move bore all the hallmarks of Freda's persuasive powers. On returning to Delhi she persuaded Nehru (with whom she was particularly close) to send more government help to the Kashmiri refugees, which he duly did. Freda was never bashful about pulling the most powerful strings she could to achieve her goals—a trait that continued throughout the rest of her life.

Srinagar may have stopped the marauding hordes of warrior tribesmen from entering its gates, but they were never far away, threatening the most savage killing and maiming imaginable. Freda was particularly vulnerable. BPL was far away in Delhi, working to reopen the trade lifeline, shut since the war, which was essential to Kashmir's economy. So she was alone with Ranga and Kabir, with only Rufus the Great Dane to guard them.

To protect herself and her family, Freda did the unthinkable. She took up arms by joining a women's militia—the Women's Self-Defence Corps—started by some feisty members of the Communist Party affiliated with Sheikh Abdullah's National Conference Party. They demanded to be trained and given arms in the face of the countless women being raped, abducted, and killed all around them. For Freda, a follower of Gandhi, it was a radical but necessary step. She spent hours drilling on a parade ground, learning to shoot a gun and lob a grenade alongside seventy other women, all volunteers gleaned from all classes, who had pledged to protect not only themselves but the citizens of Srinagar itself. This Band of Sisters broke all cultural, social, and historical traditions in the subcontinent, where women conventionally took submissive roles (in public at least). It was a big story, and was reported with pride in *The People's Age*, a newspaper to which BPL contributed.

"For the first time on the soil of India there is being built an army of women trained to use the rifle and other modern weapons of war. The women of Kashmir are the first in India to build an army of women trained to use the rifle. By their example they have made Indian history, filled our chests with pride, and raised our country's banner higher among the great nations of the world."

The writing bears all the hallmarks of BPL's communist rhetoric and with it the pledge to achieve female emancipation.

Nehru came to inspect the Women's Self-Defence Corps, and press photographs reveal Freda standing boldly upright, rifle in hand, the only white face among a sea of brown ones. The training took up hours of her precious time, but in the end she never had to shoot anyone.

By the beginning of 1949, things were quieting down a little. On January 1, a cease-fire had been established following the condemnation of the Kashmir crisis by the United Nations. The maharaja, Sir Hari Singh, had fled, and much to Freda's approval Hindus, Muslims, Sikhs, Harijans, and Christians began living peacefully side by side, in the capital at least. For the next few years, Freda and BPL got down to building up a new "enlightened" society. "Kashmir with its socialist government and its young leaders can lead India and rebuild this miserable country. I have great faith in it and love it, too. It's beautiful, rich in talent and natural resources," she claimed.

For the first (and last) time, BPL was bringing in a regular salary—employed in various capacities by Sheik Abdullah's government. Freda's portfolio was massive. Not only did she continue her work with the refugees, she also established a Houseboatmen's and Domestic Workers Unemployment Relief School, giving technical training to the children of classes hard hit by the stoppage of the lucrative tourist trade. She was delighted that the training carried with it a monthly cash payment for each child, thus enabling hard-hit families to buy food.

She and BPL also rewrote more than ninety school and college textbooks. "Kashmir was the first part of India to reorganize its teaching materials so that the books fitted in with the new world and the new free India that our children now live in," she boasted.

In a brief respite from her heavy workload, Freda managed to become pregnant again. The decision to have another child was not prompted by maternal longing, however, but the consideration that Kabir might be lonely. She wrote to Olive, "The latest family news is that we are expecting a sister (finally, a sister) for the boys in early September. It's really a lot to take on—a new baby in the midst of present-day Kashmir, but Kabir needs someone his own age—and there's a lovely garden to relax in and forget, sometimes, the quarrels and miseries of the world. So I carry on and make baby clothes. Ranga, who is slender with brown eyes and black hair, is now head boy at Hadow School and takes his matriculation examination next year. Kabir is in kindergarten." (How Freda knew that her unborn baby would be female is unknown.)

On September 15, 1949, Freda gave birth to a girl. They called her Gulhima (shortened to Guli), meaning "Rose of the Snows," a fitting name, Freda thought, for a child born in the valley of the Himalayas, famed for its snow, flowers, and gardens. "She's a happy, independent little being, with golden hair and black eyes," she said.

Never one to forsake her calling for motherhood, the very next year, Freda was back at work, this time as a member of the Board of English and Philosophic Studies at the newly founded Jammu and Kashmir University. By the autumn of 1950, she had taken on the additional role of visiting professor in the pioneering college, newly established in Srinagar especially for Kashmiri girls wanting to get their BA or BS degrees. She worked late into the night, diligently marking all the papers.

"We hope to produce our first graduates by the summer of 1952. There are 160 girls studying at the college, which is quite a good number for a part of the world where in the old days everything was done to discourage rather than encourage higher education for women," she said.

More work was in store. In 1950, all of North India suffered the most dreadful floods. Freda became Secretary of the Government Flood Relief Committee for Srinagar and Suburbs. In the same year, both Kabir and Guli contracted whooping cough. Despite all this, she could still see the bright side. "The mountains and lakes are full of mysterious mists and colors. Living on the edge of one of the world's volcanoes has its compensations," she told Olive.

There was time for a social life. Freda was very highly regarded throughout Kashmir, and with their connections the Bedis became a celebrated couple, frequenting many high-society cocktail parties.

"Mrs. Bedi was a very fine woman, striking-looking, very modest, and very well known throughout the valley in Kashmir," said Pran Nath Jalali, a fellow sister in the Women's Self-Defence Corps, who counted the Bedis among her friends. "BPL was a very funny character, a happy-go-lucky type. I never saw him brooding. You could approach him anytime, and you were welcome."

The Bedis' house, with its beautiful gardens bordering on Dal Lake and its open-door policy, became a magnet for many business-people, international holidaymakers, educators, and journalists alike, including the celebrated American photojournalist Margaret Bourke-White, of *Life* magazine fame. "She was an elderly lady, yet she hung on telegraph poles to get her story," remembered Ranga.

In spite of her extraordinary workload, her husband, and her children, Freda still pursued her spiritual quest, trying to find a path that would fulfill all her deepest yearnings for ultimate Truth and Freedom. Her search was exceptionally meticulous. Following her nonsectarian bent, she decided to take one religion at a time and study it thoroughly. For one year she practiced Islam, praying five times a day and observing the feast days. When a Canadian Jewish professor and his wife visited Kashmir, she studied Judaism with a green-leather-bound Torah that they gave her. Then she observed the Hindu fasts and studied the gods; Shiva, Ganesh, Krishna—all were equally important to her. And, of course, she became thoroughly acquainted with Sikhism, the religion of her husband's forefathers.

One day she met a Tibetan Buddhist lama in Srinagar, the head of a Ladakhi monastery visiting from the other side of the continent. It was a brief encounter, but something resonated deeply within Freda. "She felt it was special, somehow. To me he was only a blur of robes," said Kabir.

By 1951, the thorny political issue of offering the people of Kashmir a plebiscite to let them decide whether they wanted to join Pakistan or accede to India hung heavily in the air. Freda was torn. While she believed in the people's right to choose, she was adamantly against Pakistan's propaganda, with its call for Islamic separation and the holocaust she feared would irrevocably follow, with Hindus and Sikhs the losers.

"There will be a tough fight when and if a plebiscite takes place. The other side uses low weapons—an appeal to religious fanaticism and hatred, which can always find a response. We fight with clean hands. I am content as a democrat that Kashmir should vote and turn whichever way it wishes, but I know a Pakistan victory would mean massacre and mass migration of Hindus and Sikhs—and I hate to face it. God forbid it should happen," she said.

For the first time she revealed an anticommunist leaning. "I feel the British Press—with the exception of our friend Norman Cliff on the *News Chronicle*—is Pakistan minded, and while I realize that Pakistan and Middle East oil interests are linked, I think it is a great injustice to Kashmir. While a very brutal invasion and a lot of propaganda from the Pakistan side has been trying to make the state communist minded, it has valiantly stuck to its democratic ideas and built up this very war-torn, hungry world."

BPL was valiantly doing his part in promoting counterpropaganda (a role given to him by Sheik Abdullah's administration), churning out publicity and articles both in Delhi and in Kashmir. One day in 1952, things went catastrophically wrong. BPL had a huge argument with his old friend Sheikh Abdullah, who was about to make a speech ratifying the plebiscite.

Kabir said, "My father warned him that India would never accept such a move and that Sheikh Abdullah would be jailed. He was also afraid that a plebiscite would deepen the split already existing in the state and would destroy the work that he, Mummy, and others had been carefully building up over the fragile early years to promote harmony and improve the living conditions of *all* the people. Kashmir had a huge Muslim majority, but anti-Pakistan feeling was also very high in Kashmir. That was what my father was working with, especially with his counterpropaganda. His ultimate commitment and hope was that Kashmir would be joined to secular India, with its democratic principles. Sadly the best of friendships ended in a bitter battle."

The minute his argument with Sheikh Abdullah was over, BPL went home, packed up all his household goods and his family, and within twenty-four hours had moved everyone to Delhi. He could no longer stay in a Kashmir that he felt was heading for trouble, and in the employ of a man whose policies he no longer believed in. His prediction was right. In 1953, Sheik Abdullah was dismissed as prime minister, arrested on charges of conspiracy against the state, and jailed for eleven years. In Delhi, BPL never stopped petitioning for his release.

It was a rude departure from the Kashmir that they loved and had served for over five years, and carried a sour whiff of rancor about it. Nevertheless, Freda was proud of the legacy she had left behind.

"A great deal has been done to change the feudal face of this traditionally backward area. Land legislation has been given to the tiller of the soil, all absentee landlordism has been abolished, and the landlord left with twenty-two acres, his orchards, and trees so that he may live a decent but not exploitative life. Trade has been canalized into emporiums, which are now all over India, thanks to BPL's work, bringing in much-needed revenue to the gifted artists and craftsmen of Kashmir. A larger part of the state budget has been given to education than in almost any other part of India. We have a very dynamic Education Ministry, and we cut through red tape and get things done much more quickly. A plan to establish youth hostels, recreation centers, and youth camps is also under way."

She could have added many more achievements to her list, not least her pioneering work in giving equal opportunities to women.

Freda and BPL had certainly left their mark on Kashmir, but the contentious issue of to whom it belonged was not resolved—and the argument continues to this day.

Once again Freda and her family were stepping into the unknown.

The dates listed here are approximate.

1948. Freda totes a gun as a member of The Women's Self-Defence Corps in the bloody aftermath of Partition—a radical step for an advocate of non-violence. Pictured with Ranga, Kabir, and the family's Great Dane, Rufus. (Bedi family archives.)

1946. Children Kabir and Ranga with their mom in the Lahore meadows surrounding the straw and mud huts where the family lived a back-to-nature existence until Independence. Freda was in heaven. (Bedi family archives.)

1947. Back in England, Freda introduces Kabir to her mother, Nellie, and brother John. (Bedi family archives.)

1950. The first appearance of Freda's daughter Gulhima, "Rose of the Snows," born in Kashmir on September 15, 1949. Pictured with her brother Kabir, in front of their more conventional house. (Bedi family archives.)

1960. Freda, BPL, Kabir, and Guli on the steps of their small Delhi flat with newly "adopted" family members, Chögyam Trungpa Rinpoche and Akong Rinpoche, found by Freda in the refugee camps. They lived together for several years. (Bedi family archives.)

1961. Freda, still a career woman, in Delhi with her two favorite protégées: Chögyam Trungpa Rinpoche (left) and Akong Rinpoche (right). (Bedi family archives.)

1963. The Young Lamas Home School, Dalhousie, India. Freda with the reincarnated Tibetan lamas she was educating in English and modern history to bring Buddhism to the outside world. (Courtesy Faith Grahame.)

1963. One of the many Western volunteers teaches outside the Young Lamas Home School, Dalhousie, India. (Bedi family archives.)

1963. "With my Lama son, Trungpa Tulku." Freda, still in lay clothes, with Chögyam Trungpa Rinpoche. (Bedi family archives.)

1966. The Bedi family with Freda finally in her Buddhist robes and with a shaved head. Transition complete. (Bedi family archives.)

9

Turning Point

THE ABRUPT dislocation from their lakeside home, with its backdrop of snowcapped mountains, to the teeming, hot, dusty, dirty cityscape of Delhi was a rude shock. The Bedis were broke, homeless, and without work. Furthermore, Freda had four-year-old Guli and six-year-old Kabir to look after. Ranga was already in Delhi, a BA student in History and Economics at St. Stephen's College.

In desperation, the Bedis initially fell back on their tried-and-tested practice of camping instead of buying or renting. On the outskirts of the bustling capital was a walled area of about five acres belonging to a friend of Freda's, the White Maharani of Patiala (in the Punjab). Part of the land was taken up by the Ashoka Vihara Center, a community of monks, but the rest was open ground, some of it containing ruins. It was much to their liking.

The Bedi tents had style. They were large with mesh windows to stop the mosquitoes, and beautiful Kashmiri rugs on the floor (on loan from the Maharani). Their neighbors were a motley collection of eccentric, colorful characters. For Guli and Kabir it was a magic playground. They cooked pigeon over communal fires, and made friends with all the stray dogs. As adults, they admitted their upbringing may have been precarious, even dangerous, but it was never dull.

Finding work was the next necessity. After his experience in Kashmir, BPL claimed he was incapable of working under anyone, but was perpetually optimistic that life would provide. He settled down to translate into English the mystic poetry of Guru Gobind Singh (the last of the ten Sikh gurus) and Bhai Nand Lal (a seventeenth-century Persian and Arabic poet of the Punjab)—and to research Eastern religions.

It fell to Freda yet again to become the principal breadwinner. She could have had her pick of top, high-paying political positions (her CV was impressive, her reputation enormous, and her connections the very best). Instead she chose a government job as editor of *Social Welfare*, the organ of the Central Social Welfare Board, part of the Ministry of Education. *Social Welfare* was written in English and translated into Hindi to reach as many people as possible. She chose with her heart—still wanting to help the poor and needy. The pay was low, but with her job came a government apartment.

"It was horrible," said Kabir. "It was in a colony on the outskirts of the city—with a terrace where we slept and very cheap cement flooring with flecks in it. We all crammed in—Mummy, Papa, Guli, me, Granny, who was bedridden by this stage, and the Great Dane. The irony was that Papa had acquired a grand secondhand Packard (reputedly it had once belonged to Gandhi), which Papa absolutely adored. But he had no money to repair or maintain it, so it just stayed outside on the street. He also built a chicken coop in the backyard so he could have a fresh supply of his beloved eggs. I remember one day Mummy came home to find not a single fowl in the yard. 'Bedi, where are the chickens?' she asked. 'Freda, one of them got sick and I had to kill them all!' he replied. Then she noticed the kitchen was full of jars of chicken pickle, and she knew. Papa made the best chicken pickle imaginable."

Once again Freda's workload was immense. Her mandate was to coordinate and report on the many social welfare programs in place throughout the subcontinent. This meant, in effect, traveling from Kerala, in the southernmost tip, to Himachal Pradesh, in the north, overseeing new enterprises that she helped instigate as well as mentoring a band of volunteer social workers. The work was demanding and she loved it.

"I always make a particular point of wandering about villages to our more remote welfare extension projects to understand at firsthand the problems of village workers. I aim to promote women's literacy, as well as teaching them handicrafts, helping them in childbirth and in child upbringing, as well as running nursery schools and child recreation groups. This sort of work everybody needs as it re-creates the basic village, which is the cornerstone of India's economy," she said.

"It is rough going in jeeps, but great fun too. I can never get over the feeling that it is relatively more important to see what is happening in places that the 'Big' people all over the world rarely penetrate, than to see the larger and much-visited institutions at the city level."

Kabir, who sometimes accompanied Freda on these excursions, observed, "Mummy had more than a social conscience, she cared intimately about everyone. She became part of their lives. She helped people over and over again. She saw people's inner virtues. Her job as editor of *Social Welfare* was much more than journalism. Her writings became a record of social conditions across India and a mouthpiece for social change and encouragement."

This tremendous work effort, the building up of yet another career path, and her heroic achievement in settling her family yet again into a different way of life was about to be dramatically overturned. In 1953, shortly after arriving in Delhi, Nehru sent Freda to Burma as the Indian representative of a UNESCO mission. For the first time in her life Freda found herself in a rich and exclusively Buddhist country. The impact was immediate and galvanic. Surrounded by hundreds of pagodas and thousands of monks roaming the streets in saffron robes, she instantly felt she had come home.

"When I set foot on that soil, the Golden Temple, the monks with their begging bowls, suddenly it was déjà vu. Without understanding anything much about Buddhism, I knew. This is The Way, this is what I have been looking for. I saw the whole thing," she said. Freda was forty-two years old. Her long, diligent quest to find her true spiritual path was finally over. It had taken thirty-eight years, since her first days of sitting in her local church in Derby before school trying to meditate. Curiously, in spite of her remarkable effort and conscientiousness in searching and trying out the world's great religious traditions, she had never come across Buddhism before, even though the Buddha had been born, taught, and attained enlightenment in India. His message had thrived there for over seven hundred years, until the Mughals invaded in the thirteenth century. They had swept in from the Middle East, destroying the renowned Nalanda University, hailed as the greatest center of learning in Asia, and setting fire to the largest Buddhist library in the ancient world, which allegedly burned for three months. Thousands of Buddhist monks and scholars fled into obscurity in the Himalayan kingdoms, from where Buddhism spread to the Far East and Southeast Asia. From then on, the Buddha was incorporated into the pantheon of Hindu gods and was regarded as a mythological figure.

Burma now boasted some of the most accomplished Buddhist meditation masters on the planet. Freda wasted no time seeking them out. As usual she went straight to the top.

Sayadaw U Thittila Aggamahapandita was vice president of the World Fellowship of Buddhists and spoke excellent English. He agreed to teach Freda personally for eight weeks. The regime was tough and exceptionally rigorous, demanding she be aware of each detail involved in every activity—walking, eating, brushing teeth, putting on shoes, blinking. Every breath was accompanied by awareness. And then awareness itself was watched by awareness.

This acute investigation is called *Vipassana*, or Insight Meditation, the meditation technique of looking inward to face the inner landscape of one's mind—the response to emotional, physical, mental phenomena. It was accompanied by Loving-Kindness Meditation—starting with oneself and progressing to others, particularly enemies and the multitude of neutral people. Ultimately the process leads to awakening—the emergence from the deep sleep of ignorance that blights every sentient being until they step onto to the path of searching.

Freda learned fast, mingling her meditation training with her work commitment. "I remember Sayadaw U Pandita telling me, 'If you get a realization, or a flash, it may not be sitting on your meditation cushion in front of an image of the Buddha. It will probably be somewhere you least expect it.'"

That's precisely what happened. Freda had what she called her enlightenment experience "while I was walking with the Commission through the streets of Kyaukme, in northern Burma. Suddenly I saw the flow of things, the meaning and the connection. It was the first real flash of understanding. I can't explain exactly what it was because it was beyond words. But it opened so many gates and showed me things I'd been trying to find for a very long time," she explained. She revealed to a few close friends that her Damascene experience had lasted for hours and was accompanied by great bliss.

A window had been opened, a transcendental window giving a glimpse into another reality. The aftershock was dramatic. "We got a phone call back in Delhi that Mummy had collapsed and we had to bring her home from Burma immediately," says Ranga. "Of course we had no money, so we went around to Nehru and Indira's house and they provided the plane fare to fetch her home and an ambulance to meet her at the airport." Continuing her tour was now out of the question.

"When she arrived, it was shocking. Mummy didn't recognize anyone. For weeks she stayed in her bed, getting up just to go to the bathroom. That's as far as she would go. She wouldn't talk or register anything in the outside world. She'd eat the food put in front of her like an automaton. If you looked at her, it was like looking into a stone wall. She never saw you. It was as though she were catatonic. It was terrifying for all of us—except Papa. He didn't seem concerned at all. He said it was all happening as it should and that it would work out all right. He was correct. After about six weeks she began to show signs of improvement. Her face became more expressive and she began to interact with us. But it took about three months before she was back to normal."

Gradually she resumed her work and tried to get back to her old life, but she had irrevocably changed. After Burma she was going in a different direction, and nothing was going to be the same. The first to feel the impact was BPL. Their marriage of twenty years had been founded on love, intellectual compatibility, and their shared vision of an independent India. That last job had been completed. Freda knew with certainty that that phase of her life was over. Her heart and her path now belonged to the Buddha.

She calmly sat her husband down and announced, "I've been searching all my life, but it's the Buddhist monks who have been able to show me what it is that I have been looking for. I am a Buddhist from now on—and I have taken a personal vow of a brahmacharya," she said, referring to the vow of celibacy said to induce spiritual purity and enhance one's capacity for divine happiness.

BPL took the news remarkably well. His relationship with Freda had always been based on tolerance and respect for each other's strong but different personalities. And the right to personal freedom was a tenet they held dear, both on a personal and on a political level.

Kabir explains, "It was a very good marriage. There were occasional arguments, but never any serious rows in our house, although Mummy could get exasperated with Papa—with his collecting of small animals that grew into very large ones, for example. There was no doubt that they were both the loves of each other's lives. Papa accepted Mummy's choice and, as far as I can remember, was not resentful at all. I don't think there was ever a spiritual separation between them."

Another reason that BPL took Freda's news with such equanimity was that his inner life was running along parallel lines. For some time he had been following his own spiritual quest and was undergoing his own enlightenment experience. It bore all the hallmarks of his originality. "He would sit still for hours without moving. He would babble in voices we didn't understand. He'd go up onto the roof and stand for hours with his arms outstretched toward a shrine of a Sufi saint," said Kabir. "We called the doctor, but Papa just smiled at him. 'What I'm going through is beyond you,' he told him. The doctor nevertheless insisted on examining him. 'You won't find a pulse,' said Papa. He was right. The astonished doctor left.

"Father started going on walks, discovering the graves of Sufi saints in the area, telling us where they were, both marked and unmarked. He started to do automatic writing. Word got out and people started coming to the house with their problems. Papa would listen, then begin writing, and eventually hand them sheets of paper with answers to their troubles on them. In time he became quite a healer and was known as Baba Bedi, the name given to a holy man."

By the late 1950s and early 1960s, the first of the hippies and the Beat Generation were arriving in India, and many found their way to BPL's door. "Then the house got full of really strange people. Papa always made it quite clear to all of them, however, that he was not a saint, nor was he going to behave like one. 'I'll smoke my cigarettes and drink my whiskey as normal—and not be bound by anyone,' Papa said. Gradually he stopped writing automatic messages and started speaking words that had begun coming through him. At first his voice and way of talking were strange, but then the style evolved and he talked like himself," said Kabir.

The family noticed a subtle, definite change in Freda after her Burma experience. "She was calmer," said Ranga. "Mummy was always rather highly strung and could get impatient if people didn't grasp things immediately. Not that she was ever harsh. After Burma she was 'softer,' and took time to explain. When Father emerged from his religious experience, there was no change at all!"

The next event to send shock waves through the family was when Freda, for reasons of her own, sent Guli to boarding school miles away in North India. Her daughter was just five years old. It seemed not only cruel but a terrible dereliction of maternal duty, and out of character with her essentially kind, caring nature. In addition, she performed the deed in what appeared a particularly brutal way.

Guli, now a tall, sociable woman who has dedicated her life to teaching children with special needs, lives in Nashua, New Hampshire, outside Boston, Massachusetts. She recalls every detail of the traumatic event. "When Mummy told me her idea, I told her outright, 'I am not going to boarding school!' We children were all strong characters, who had been taught to speak up. She arranged everything extremely well. We often went touring, and this year Mummy took me to visit an old family friend, Auntie Mera (who had adopted thirteen children) in Naina Tal, in the foothills of Uttar Pradesh. When we got there, she asked if I wanted to see All Saints School, which was nearby and run by Christian nuns. I said yes. I remember the oak tree in the garden, which was huge, and I got very animated and chatty with the nuns. I turned around to tell Mummy something and she was gone. I was absolutely devastated. I cried for three days. The nuns, British Anglican missionaries, were so kind. They really cared for me."

Guli grew to love her school. "It turned out to be the best experience. I studied the scriptures and I know *everything* about the Bible. I loved the hymns and the feeling of the chapel, not that I ever felt the need to become a Christian. There was never any talk about conversion! Of course, I missed my mother and I think she felt a little bad. She wrote to me every week. I always got a letter. I could count on it. And when I did return to the family on the holidays, I was always happy to hop on the train to go back to school. When I was older and Mummy had moved to Dalhousie, she asked if I wanted to change schools to be near her and I said no. I didn't want to leave. I think she was a little browned off."

Still, the puzzlement of why Freda had sent her away at such a young age remained. It resurfaced with a vengeance when Guli became a mother herself. Finally she confronted Freda directly. "When I first had a baby of my own, I could not understand how she could have done it. I was just five years old, for heaven's sake! I wrote to her bluntly: 'What an amazing mother! With all of your spiritual and religious convictions, how could you forsake your child?' She never really acknowledged it. 'I got your letter—thank you,' was her only reply.

"Later she answered me properly in person. 'You never understood why I sent you to boarding school. I was a social worker for many years and I witnessed the absolute tragedy of young girls sexually molested by servants and family members. Your father was a loving man, but he didn't understand these things. I was afraid he'd leave you alone when I was not there to protect you. That's the reason I sent you to boarding school."

Guli totally accepted her mother's reasoning. "I got it. By then I'd come across many cases of abused kids myself. Thankfully, I was never sexually abused," she said.

To all outer appearances, life in Delhi continued as usual for the Bedi household: Freda working all hours, BPL doing freelance writing, the two younger children being educated at their respective schools, Ranga now grown up and following his chosen career in tea. As usual, money was frighteningly scarce, and the family's living arrangements were haphazard.

"I never had a settled family home. In Delhi the family moved from government flat to government flat, so that when I came back from boarding school, I never knew where I was going to live. The longest I stayed anywhere was a year," said Guli. "And we were always broke. My father was a wonderful man but he had a devil-may-care attitude of 'the money will come.' He was a truly free spirit, and the most optimistic person I ever met. He was super-bright, charismatic, and had a presence. I could see why Mummy fell in love with him. Papa never wore a responsible hat in his life. Now I feel like kicking him.

"Then I look at Mummy. She had to pay school fees and feed us. Mummy had to work so hard. I don't know how she did it. Her life was *real*—it wasn't all 'ha-ha-he-he.' I remember one Christmas, which we always celebrated, I really wanted a paint set. It cost fifty rupees. Mummy said she couldn't afford it. I wept. I'd never heard her say she had no money before. But once Christmas arrived, there it was under the tree. The strain she went through . . ." said Guli.

"They were very loving parents, and we were taught to love everyone. They ran a very generous home. Whatever they had, they gave. One day we came home and found we'd been robbed. The thieves had taken all of Mummy's saris. 'It's OK, darlings,' she said. 'Whoever did this needed it more than we do.' Mrs. Gandhi used to give her the most elegant, beautiful saris, but she would often give them away. 'Some poor little girl in the office needs it,' she'd say."

Financially they were poor, but the Bedis' social life among artists, writers, diplomats, politicians, and hippies was exceedingly rich. Freda's connection with Prime Minister Nehru and his daughter, Indira, remained strong, and the couple and the young Bedi children were frequent visitors to their house.

"We shared their box at the India Independence Day parades, and were invited to Indira's sons' birthday parties," said Kabir. "Sanjay and Rajiv had a room just for their toys. They filled the entire room—electric trains, Meccano—all gifts from foreign dignitaries. They also had two dogs, Pepe and Maddho. Pepe once bit Guli on the bottom!" he recalled with a laugh.

"Mummy never took advantage of the friendship. She never asked for anything. We were seven years waiting for a telephone line—all she had to do was whisper to Indira and we'd have got six telephones. But she wouldn't do it. That's why Indira trusted her," he said.

Freda was certainly never a snob, nor did she ever forsake her socialist principles. The family members vividly recall the occasion when the Burmese ambassador and other diplomats had been invited to dinner and the doorbell rang. It was a servant who had been with them for many years but who came and went as he pleased. This time he had been away for over a year and was expecting to get his job back. Freda let him in, pulled up an extra chair at the table, and sat him next to the ambassador.

For all her full secular and social life Freda still found time to practice the meditation she had learned with Sayadaw U Pandita. Having found her true path, she was not going to let it go. Whenever she could, she traveled to Burma to continue her meditation training under his strict, watchful eye. Sometimes she took Kabir, her "special child" with her, encouraging him to shave his head and don Buddhist robes as a child monk. Secretly she hoped that one day he would be ordained. That destiny was not to be his, however.

10

Meeting the Tibetans

ON MARCH 31, 1959, burdened by grief, exhaustion, and illness, the Fourteenth Dalai Lama of Tibet left his homeland forever and stepped into exile in India. He had only left at the urgings of Nechung, the State Oracle of Tibet, who had guided successive Dalai Lamas through the medium-ship of trance. A unique institution, the Tibetan government took no major decisions without first consulting the oracle. Now the oracle pronounced his life in dire danger and that he could do more to help his beleaguered people if he made their plight known to the outside world. His escape out of Tibet had been hazardous, traversing the highest mountain ranges on earth with the Chinese troops hot on his heels. Finally he reached the sanctuary of India; the Buddha's birthplace was willing to give him refuge.

Prime Minister Nehru, prompted by his daughter Indira (who possibly had been prompted by Freda), graciously extended the twenty-four-year-old spiritual and temporal leader of Tibet a warm welcome on the grounds that India and Tibet shared cultural and spiritual bonds that had existed for centuries. Back in Tibet word quickly got out that the Dalai Lama was not dead, as rumored, but was alive and living in India, whereupon thousands of monks and laypeople promptly abandoned their homes, gathered up a few possessions, and followed their revered leader into exile. They were following not just a leader but a person they believed was the embodiment of the Buddha of Compassion, a figure who would preserve their unique Buddhist way of life, which was currently being systematically destroyed by the invading Revolutionary Chinese forces. The Tibetan diaspora had begun.

They arrived in India traumatized, starving, ill, filthy, and utterly disoriented. Their escape to freedom had been pitted with unimaginable horror—snow, ice, crevasses that suddenly opened up under their feet, and Chinese troops who shot on sight. They had seen many of their countrymen lose their lives. Not sure what to do with this great influx of lost, battered humanity, Nehru sent for the one person whom he knew was qualified to help: Freda Bedi. Nehru knew from firsthand knowledge that she had handled the refugee crisis in Kashmir after Partition with consummate skill, was an excellent administrator, and furthermore was currently engaged in social work throughout the subcontinent. He'd also heard she had a newfound affinity with Buddhism. He duly appointed her adviser on Tibetan refugees in the Ministry of External Affairs. She readily agreed.

A letter she wrote to Olive, however, suggested that it was she who had subtly put the idea into Nehru's head. "I felt that as a Buddhist and part of the Social Welfare Board—with a particular interest in women and children—I might have some role in helping to rehabilitate them and the lamas. Pandit Nehru agreed that a woman's eye might be useful."

She immediately headed for Missamari and Buxa in West Bengal, where the majority of refugees had been accommodated. T. C. Tethong, later private secretary to the Dalai Lama, was a twenty-four-year-old Tibetan studying medicine in nearby Darjeeling when the Dalai Lama crossed into India. He was called upon to act as interpreter from Tibetan to English and vividly recalls Freda's arrival on the scene. "The first time she came to help, she was in such a hurry that she hadn't got the necessary permit to enter the camps—which were designated a restricted area because of the delicate political situation. So she returned with the right documentation and after assessing the situation got down to work. She was a great humanitarian. All those who knew her respected her enormously. She helped whomever she could, whenever she could—continually struggling to keep pressuring the right people for aid."

The situation that Freda found herself in was overwhelming and chaotic. Contractors were working day and night frantically erecting bamboo huts that could house fifty to seventy refugees each. Initially there were over seven thousand people, nearly all men—monks, government officials, and freedom fighters. But T. C. Tethong also remembered among the throng a Chinese military man and his family who had been posted to Tibet and who took the opportunity to escape too. The second wave of refugees came through Nepal, Bhutan, Sikkim, Ladakh, and Kinnaur. Places had to be found for them all. Many were sent to settlements in South India. They kept pouring in, their numbers rising from thirty thousand to seventy thousand.

It was a grim, pitiful, and overwhelming sight that greeted Freda on her arrival. The Tibetans were ill, starving, disoriented, and highly traumatized. Their journey out had been long and fraught with danger. They staggered into India wearing their unsuitable heavy wool, fur, and leather clothes, now stinking and thick with grime, and found an alien world, as frightening as the one they had left behind.

To begin with, the climate was unbearably hot for people born and raised on the clean, clear, cold air of the Tibetan plateau. Used to eating yak meat and barley (the only foods their terrain could sustain), their stomachs could not digest the rice, vegetables, and hot spices—the subsistence food offered to them. Nor could they safely drink the water, which had an unusually high iron content. Consequently they became sick, picking up tropical diseases and, worst of all, tuberculosis, which spread like wildfire among them.

It is unknown whether Freda recognized the irony that the great socialist ideal that she and her husband espoused had caused the greatest suffering the Tibetan people had ever known, destroying their most precious possession—their unique religion, the faith that Freda now proudly called her own.

Freda rolled up her sleeves and got down to work, moving between the camps at Missamari, Buxa, Sikkim, and Kalimpong. She worked around the clock, greeting the newcomers with cups of tea and words of comfort, tending to their sores and sicknesses, and trying to soothe their emotional scars. To the refugees she must have been an unlikely sight. Tibet had been locked to outsiders for centuries, and its inhabitants had never seen a Westerner before. Moreover, they had been taught to view them all as barbarians, "red-skinned devils," primitive beings who had not been refined by the Buddhadharma. Now they opened their hearts to the tall, fair-skinned Freda, who was helping them so selflessly. As one they began to call her "Mummy" and then "Mummy-la" (this suffix being a mark of high esteem).

Freda was moved. She learned that within Tibetan culture the figure of the mother (any mother) was universally held in the highest regard, even reverence. The mother was the person who brought forth life, nourished that life with her own body, and was prepared to sacrifice her own life for the sake of her child. In short, the mother was the highest example on earth of selfless love. Freda was ready to take on the title. "Technically I was welfare adviser to the Ministry; in actuality I was Mother to a camp full of soldiers, lamas, peasants, and families. Women and children were barely thirteen hundred in number, but how precious they were, for on them depended the continuance of the old Tibetan culture. We struggled with commercial baby formula and barley to save the babies, whose mothers' milk had dried up on the escape or as a result of their suffering. Others had worms or diseases contracted during the arduous journey. There were no office hours. Sunrise was the signal for the first visitors," Freda wrote to Olive.

"We had no electricity, so work slowed down when dark came. But even after that, we used to go round the barracks and into the hospitals with volunteers and interpreters to pick up the sick and solve the day's problems. I can't begin to tell you of the tragic stories all carried in their hearts. We even avoided inquiring, so that old wounds would not be torn open again, and gave instead positive hopes of work and resettlement. Much of my time was spent keeping friends and family groups together when the dispersal to work sites and centers was taking place. For those who have lost home, country, and almost every possession, family and village ties are all that is left, and they assume tremendous importance and significance."

The Tibetans were scrutinizing the unaccustomed personage of a white woman, and Freda in turn was certainly regarding them. She, like other Westerners, had never come across Tibetans or their culture. Secreted away within their mighty Himalayan fortress, the forbidden country of Tibet had remained a mystery to the rest of the world for centuries. In 1959 that isolationist policy had been rudely crushed, and the Tibetans were thrust out into the world. Their appearance may have been dirty and bedraggled, their bodies broken, and their demeanor utterly disoriented, but Freda was deeply and immediately struck by a certain quality she had not encountered before.

It was Mahayana Buddhism, which is based on love, kindness, and compassion toward all, even your enemies. Over the centuries it had seeped into the very soil of Tibet and the bones of its inhabitants and had now come to their aid in their greatest hour of need. For the Mahayanist, nirvana, the liberation of self from the cycle of endless births and death, was not enough. For how could you stay in the bliss of heaven while countless others were still suffering in ignorance, they argued? The followers of Mahayana instead vowed to relinquish liberation until all beings were freed. And so they hung their prayer flags on mountaintops so that the wind could carry their messages to beings in all ten directions, and they spun their prayer wheels for the benefit of all, and every day they uttered their wish that every living creature be free from sorrow and live in lasting peace and happiness.

While average Tibetans stopped there in their religious activity, the lamas coupled this altruistic intention with profound scholarship and an extraordinary panoply of meditation techniques set down for them to follow in order to achieve their goal of universal enlightenment. The truly dedicated set off to remote mountain caves where they meditated in isolation for years, even decades. As a result Tibet produced an unprecedented number of enlightened beings, almost on a conveyor belt. It was their finest accomplishment, and now their gift to the world.

Freda had not experienced anything like it. In the refugees Freda found no traces of bitterness, resentment, or anger, only a reinforcement of their prayers. This resonated deeply with Freda's own innate compassionate nature and her newly awakened Buddhist path. "Every morning and night, the chanting of incredibly soothing and rhythmical prayers of the lamas filled the air. Each home group had its private shrine, and butter lamps were burned, even if rations had to be sacrificed. Their piety and devotion meant more to them than bread," said Freda. "The Tibetans are honest, brave, and wonderful people. The five thousand lamas we have inherited contain some of the most remarkable, spiritually advanced monks and teachers it has been my privilege to meet."

Freda's spiritual life was a juggernaut now gathering momentum. Soon it would not be merely an important component of her life—it would become her whole life.

Freda, who clearly did not believe in sheltering her children from the harsh realities of life, especially when others were in trouble, took both Kabir and Guli to work with her in the refugee camps during their school holidays. It was a harsh wake-up call, even for children who were used to precarious situations. "It was shocking," said Guli. "People's noses were falling off from frostbite. There was such suffering. Everything was overwhelming, especially the smell. The Indian government was doing its best, but it was a truly chaotic, critical situation."

"Conditions were terrible," said Kabir. "I was put to work swabbing wounds, even though I had no medical training. I would also do trips back to Delhi to visit relief agencies to get more help, armed with the names from Mummy of who she knew could donate. There were no bandages, medicines, or anything. In fact, I myself came down with tuberculosis. Mummy treated everyone, but she had a special affinity for the women and children. She told me that it was the women who had held the men together on the march out. They were the stronger sex, but when they settled in India, they collapsed and the men took over."

Eventually, after months of working all hours in appalling conditions through the various camps, the strain took its toll. Freda, always finely tuned and highly sensitive, suffered another collapse and was hospitalized.

"It was serious," said Guli. "I was taken out of boarding school and so was Kabir to visit her at the Willingdon Nursing Home in Delhi. It was quite luxurious, with air-conditioning, so I think Mrs. Gandhi may have arranged it. She was suffering from complete mental and physical exhaustion. The doctors felt she would pull through if she saw our faces. I remember that all the shades were drawn. I sat on one side of the bed and Kabir on the other. Father said, 'The children are here,' and she opened her eyes and squeezed my hand. It was the first sign of life she'd shown. The next day she was sitting up in bed, on the road to recovery.

"The problem was she couldn't stand what she was seeing. She *had* to do something about it, and it had reached a point where she couldn't handle it anymore. Mummy never allowed herself any comfort—she always lived like the people. It was part of her personal ethos. She'd always travel third class, for example, and lived in huts and tents. At one level she had enormous fortitude, but she was also fragile. And she worked so hard. She never stopped."

When she was better, she returned to work with added zeal.

One day while she was working in Sikkim, the beautiful country bordering Nepal, dubbed one of the last Himalayan Shangri-las, she paid a visit to an old family friend, Apa Pant, an Indian diplomat stationed there. He told her she could not possibly leave without meeting the Karmapa, who had just arrived from Tibet. Freda had never heard of the Karmapa, nor had any idea of the towering figure he was within the Tibetan Buddhist hierarchy, revered and respected by all. The meeting was to seal her Buddhist destiny and determine the entire course of the rest of her life.

Many years later, she told the story in a radio interview in New York, conducted by the renowned author and religious scholar Lex Hixon.

"'Who is the Karmapa?' I asked Apa Pant. 'He's a very wonderful lama, but he lives way out in the country in a monastery in Rumtek. There's no road, so you will have to ride there.' 'That's no problem,' I replied. 'I am used to riding in the mountains.' I got hold of some ponies and a good interpreter and set off into the hills.

"We had been riding for about three hours when we saw a horse coming toward us, with a richly colored Tibetan carpet on its back.

It was the Karmapa's tea-giver, a bearded monk whose job it was to be constantly on hand to pour the Karmapa's tea. He'd been sent word that we were on our way and had ridden out to meet us. He laid out the carpet, we dismounted, and I had the most delicious salt butter tea, which I'd never tasted before, and biscuits. Already the feeling of Rumtek began to come through.

"We rode along the most enchanting path, through a forest, by a stream, until we came to the monastery. It was a tiny wooden cottage that had been built by one of the Karmapa's former incarnations, now tumbled down with hardly any paint on it, and looking all the more beautiful for that. I was taken upstairs to a little attic, and there was the Karmapa sitting on a high brocade floor cushion. He was surrounded by religious Tibetan cloth paintings (*tangkas*), and lots of birds in cages who were singing their hearts out. (Later I came to realize that birds were his signature—he just loves them. They sing a lot in his presence).

"I had a wonderful talk with him, mainly about refugee matters and what I could do to help, but then I found myself getting onto the subject of meditation. At that point in my life I was feeling very sad because the gates of Burma had been shut and I was cut off from my Burmese gurus who were teaching me Vipassana. I felt like an orphan, alone and abandoned—separated by an impenetrable bamboo curtain, with them on one side and me on the other. I turned to the Karmapa and said, 'I feel attracted to saying mantras and telling the beads, but how can I keep up my awareness meditation, Vipassana?' The Karmapa replied, 'Oh, just be mindful of the beads.' It was, of course, the perfect answer."

Toward the end of the interview, in an almost throwaway line, Freda delivered a bombshell. "As I got ready to leave, he stood up and manifested himself to me as the Buddha. It was the first time he did it. He stood in the corner of the room with one hand raised in blessing, like you see in the exquisite Gandhara Buddha sculptures. He did it quite naturally, and flash! Again, like it happened in Burma. I saw it. From then on, he was in my heart as the special one. It just happened, and how strange it was, too."

His Holiness Gyalwa Karmapa Rangjung Rigpe Dorje, was head

of one of the four schools of Tibetan Buddhism, the Kagyu, and was regarded as a spiritual giant by all people of Tibet. He was currently in his sixteenth body, the First Karmapa, Dusum Khyenpa ("the one who knows the three times") having the distinction of being the person responsible for establishing Tibet's unique system of finding reincarnated great masters. Before he died, the First Karmapa wrote down where he intended to be reborn, and sure enough a few years later, following his instructions, the search party duly found the child who was recognized as Second Karmapa.

The Kagyus trace their lineage back to the great Indian master Tilopa (988–1069) and count among their ranks some of the greatest teachers and meditators Tibet has ever produced, among them Naropa, Marpa, and his pupil, the beloved poet-saint Milarepa. Milarepa had been a villain of the first order, murdering lots of people through the power of black magic, until he sought out Marpa, who cleansed his sins through a tyrannical regime of constructing and dismantling a series of towers, until he was clear enough to retreat to a cave to engage in profound meditation. The only food he had was nettles, so his body turned entirely green, but his mind exploded into enlightenment and his voice into glorious songs.

The Sixteenth Karmapa, now living in exile in a ramshackle monastery in Sikkim, was a powerful, illustrious figure with a strong, square face that came to a point at the crown of his head (reminiscent of the Buddha's *ushnisha*). Once again Freda had cannily, although unwittingly, managed to align herself with the highest echelons of the society. She had found her heart guru. The Karmapa in turn had found not only his first Western female disciple but an invaluable, sophisticated, well-connected bridge to the workings of the bewildering outside world. He was thirty-four, Freda was forty-nine. In time, together they were to become a major force in the historical transference of Buddhism from East to West.

In a radio interview Freda expressed the significance that finding her heart guru had for her. "We need a living guru and we train to see the Buddha in him. That gives us the water to make the seed of enlightenment grow. It was a fantastic thing that the Karmapa came into my life. Now I say the Karmapa's mantra daily: 'In all my lifetimes may I not be separated from my Guru.' When I had my first flash of realization in Burma, it completely changed my life. Up to that moment I'd been a mother, professor, social worker, writer—for the first time, in Burma I was alone. I left all that behind and was able to concentrate on this deep meditation, really concentrate. It was a shower of grace from the guru."

Believing in reincarnation, Freda felt it was only logical that she had been the Karmapa's disciple many times in previous lives, which accounted for their immediate close bond on meeting. The link was now reestablished and refreshed anew.

11

The Tulkus

BACK IN DELHI, picking up the threads of her former life, Freda's thoughts were never far from the refugees, her powerful encounter with the Karmapa, and the impact that Tibetan Buddhism had on her. "My old work, the editorial chair and much besides, draws me again, but my heart and mind are still with the Tibetans," she said. At one point during this stage of her life she had an inexplicable insight. Freda "saw" that Tibetan Buddhism would not only travel to the West but would take root there. And the ones who would bring it about would be the *tulkus*, Tibet's recognized reincarnated high lamas and spiritual masters, who held the essence of the teachings. Nobody else at this time shared her vision. On the face of it, it was a highly unlikely, even preposterous notion.

Throughout its 2,500-year history Buddhism had spread widely throughout Asia, taking on the hue of the culture it had landed in, but it had never crossed the great divide between East and West. In the early 1960s, Buddhism was still virtually unknown in the West, outside of a very small handful of scholars. There were no books, no teachers, and meditation was little known. The only Buddhist organization in Britain, for example, was the Buddhist Society in London, founded in 1924 by the judge Christmas Humphreys, which confined itself to Zen and the Theravada Schools of southern Asia. Virtually nothing was known about Tibetan Buddhism (called "lamaism"), and what was known was not liked. In the eyes of the intellectual Buddhist scholars, Tibetan Buddhism was regarded as degenerate—shrouded in the magic and mystery fostered by those shamans of the Bon religion that existed in Tibet before Buddhism took root. There was too much ritual, too much Tantra, too much mumbo jumbo. Word had got out from intrepid travelers who had penetrated the secret Land of Snows that lamas could "fly," could transform themselves into other beings, perform bilocation, leave handprints in rocks, dry wet sheets in the freezing cold by raising their body temperature at will, and "die" at will, sometimes leaving nothing behind but their robes. It was a far cry from the aesthetic, respectable, chaste lines of Zen.

Tibetan Buddhism would certainly never catch on.

There was also the matter of reincarnation itself, which in the predominantly Christian West was still regarded as heretical. People had been burned at the stake and been killed en masse (such as the Cathars) for believing such anathema. In the 1960s and 1970s reincarnation was still a taboo subject. The Tibetans, however, not only completely accepted reincarnation as a given fact of life, they went farther than any other Buddhist country by devising a system to find specific rebirths of accomplished spiritual masters who had forsaken higher states of consciousness after death in order to be reborn in an earthly body solely to continue to teach others how to reach the same exalted state they had achieved. The voluntary return to this vale of tears was seen as the highest mark of altruism, brave and noble beyond measure. These were the tulkus, titled *rinpoches*, or "Precious Ones." They were the cream of Tibetan society, revered, feted, and sometimes unwittingly used as pawns in others' games of corruption. These were the people Freda was now planning to bring to the West to plant the seeds of the Buddha's teachings into American, European, and Australian soil for the first time.

Finding the right candidates, however, posed an enormous problem. The entire community of Tibetan refugees was in total disarray, with lamas, yogis, householders, carpenters, tailors, and others mingling together in a homogenized, indistinguishable mass formerly unheard of in the conservative, strictly hierarchical society of old Tibet, where tulkus were kept apart from the hoi polloi for fear of contamination. In the diaspora *all* Tibetans were literally fighting for survival in this very foreign land. Many were living in tents made out of sacking, which did little to protect them from sun, rain, or cold; others were shunted into former concentration camps, and thousands were sent to remote mountainous areas to build roads by hand. The very idea of tulkus being sent as religious ambassadors to anywhere was unthinkable. At least India shared a common border with Tibet and certainly knew of the Buddha, but the West was another planet, populated, they believed, by spiritual "barbarians."

Undeterred by, or unaware of, these seeming obstacles Freda forged ahead with her dream. She had seen for herself what she thought were exceptional, special qualities in the handful of tulkus she had come across amid the mayhem of the camps. To her eyes they exuded an unmistakable refinement, wisdom, maturity, and dignity way beyond their years, which she was convinced would be as attractive to Westerners as it was to her. She also recognized, however, that they were trapped within a medieval world and its mind-set, which Tibet had been stuck in since Buddhism took root there in the twelfth century. For example, unexposed as they were to the march of new ideas and discoveries taking place in the outside world, all Tibetans arrived in India believing the world was flat and that the center of the universe was a mythical mountain called Mount Meru. The tulkus may have received an extraordinarily fine spiritual education, but they had no knowledge of the contemporary world nor the workings of the minds of its inhabitants.

What she felt they needed was a school. "I realized that learning English was their key to the new world. Without English they could not go on," she said in a radio broadcast in America. "There were many different kinds of tulkus, but they all existed like little queen bees in the center of a hive of monks and laypeople. They were so fixed in their old ways that I thought I had better educate them," she added, referring to the supreme deference tulkus were used to receiving. Kept apart from the rest of the monastic community, the tulkus had been clothed in rich robes, set on high thrones, and waited on by a string of attendants. This was not going to work in the outside world. Her agenda was also based on the fear that unless the tulkus received a modern education, they would eventually be cut off from the rest of their people, who were now inevitably being assimilated into the twentieth century.

Freda's first step was to talk to Prime Minister Nehru, who needed no persuasion. Education was the very first issue the Dalai Lama himself had raised with him as he stepped onto Indian soil. Mr. T. C. Tethong had been present as interpreter at that historic meeting. "I was shocked. Having just escaped from a deteriorating and desperate situation in Tibet, I thought His Holiness would discuss the political scenario and what could be done to help along those lines. But the Dalai Lama's priorities were resettlement and education for his people. In retrospect he was right. We had hardly twenty people who could speak English among the refugees. Nehru had guaranteed his help. 'Don't worry, we will look after the refugees and support their education,' he'd said. And he kept that promise."

In the autumn of 1961 the Young Lamas Home School was opened in Green Park, a new colony on the outskirts of Delhi. It was built on a pleasant piece of raised ground surrounded by a great expanse of sky, and funded by Nehru's government. Freda's initial plan was to take in twelve tulkus at a time, teach them English and Hindi, and educate them in current affairs, geography, and the workings of the world they had suddenly found themselves in. At the same time they were to continue their religious lessons and practices according to the school of Tibetan Buddhism that they belonged to. Each boy was given new robes as a welcome present and settled down to a fairly strict and structured regime, imposed by Freda.

"The number grew to about twenty young lamas—very naughty little kids and very cute," remembered Guli, who visited the Young Lamas Home School during her winter holiday from boarding school.

The British author Lois Lang-Sims, who was staying with the Bedis, recorded her own impression of the school in her book *The Presence of Tibet*. Sims was clearly convinced of the authenticity of the tulku pupils. "I marvelled at these children—that strange conjunction in them of an unconscious dignity and poise with pure childishness: the manner in which they combined an unfailing consideration for others with the expression of normal boyish high spirits. In their monkish robes and heavy boots they clattered, laughing until a bell rang for lessons or prayers and promptly called out 'good-bye' and disappeared as if promptness in obedience were a matter of course. Surely these young ones, who were believed to carry within them the virtues of bygone saints, were indeed the vehicles of that spirit which had created and informed the old Tibet."

Having founded her school Freda's next task was to recruit her tulkus. Over the following years scores of tulkus from all sects of Tibetan Buddhism passed through the Young Lamas Home School. Proving her intuition absolutely correct, many of them went on to become the founding fathers of Western Buddhism. Among them was Lama Zopa Rinpoche, who came to the Young Lamas Home School as a pitifully thin teenager suffering from tuberculosis; today he holds the lofty title of Kyabje, a lama whose realization and powers are extraordinary, and heads the FPMT (Foundation for the Preservation of the Mahayana Tradition), arguably the largest network of Buddhist centers and affiliated enterprises across all continents. There were also Gelek Rinpoche, who went on to study at Cornell University and whose students include Hollywood actors and esteemed musicians; and Tarthang Tulku, who established a publishing house as well as institutes in California, Europe, and Brazil.

And then there were two boys, Chögyam Trungpa Rinpoche and his childhood friend Akong Rinpoche, who were to play major roles not only in bringing Buddhism to the West but also in Freda's personal life. From the moment she encountered Trungpa, Freda was irresistibly drawn to him, detecting an outstanding intelligence, charisma, and what she called his "spiritual purity."

The Eleventh Trungpa, once destined to become abbot of Surmang Monastery in Kham, East Tibet, and who had over thirteen thousand people attend his enthronement, was to become one of the most eminent, dazzling, innovative, influential, and controversial Buddhist teachers in America. Apart from writing groundbreaking books, such as *Cutting Through Spiritual Materialism*, he was responsible for cofounding, with Akong Rinpoche, the first

Tibetan monastery in the West, Samye Ling, in Eskdalemuir, Scotland, and the first Buddhist university in the United States, Naropa University in Boulder, Colorado.

Akong Rinpoche, from Dolma Lhakang Monastery, also in Kham, was the second incarnation of a holy lama and a renowned physician. The two rinpoches had met when they were fourteen and had become close friends. Within their spiritual hierarchy, Trungpa was regarded as senior, having initiated a superior eleven reincarnations to Akong's two.

It was when Trungpa, in retreat, heard that his monastery had been sacked and the tomb of his predecessor, the Tenth Trungpa, opened and its remains spread around the courtyard that the two rinpoches decided it was too dangerous to stay any longer in Tibet. They arranged to escape together in April 1959.

Freda met the two young men as they literally staggered into the refugee camp. They were in a worse state than any other Tibetans she had encountered, and her heart went out to them.

Akong Rinpoche told the story of the meeting shortly before his tragic murder in Tibet in October 2013, while on a visit with the approval of the Chinese authorities. He spoke from the magnificent Samye Ling, which he had helped build and had directed after Trungpa moved to the United States. During his lifetime, Akong Rinpoche had also contributed greatly to the spread of Buddhism in the wider world, expanding Samye Ling, initiating a number of impressive long-term retreat programs for Westerners, and establishing Rokpa, an international humanitarian organization. His reputation as a healer grew, and he was particularly interested in treating people with mental health problems.

"Trungpa and I were both around twenty when we met Mummy Bedi. She was the first white person I had ever seen, and frankly I thought she had come from outer space, that she wasn't human. She took special interest in us both because of what we had gone through, although she was particularly drawn to Trungpa. I think it was because we were both in such a terrible state and we had endured one of the hardest journeys of all. She asked us lots of questions about our lives and our escape. We told her everything.

"Our escape was so hard because it was so long. We thought it would only last three months, but in the end it took ten because we took such a circuitous route avoiding the Chinese. Our route was to get to Assam through the Brahmaputra region. For four months we traveled by mule and horse, but we had to do the rest on foot—and the going was hard, because we had to hide during the day and could only travel by night. It was really dangerous—there were many high passes and raging rivers we had to cross on swinging rope bridges. The Chinese were after us because Trungpa, as a high reincarnnate lama with many followers, had a price on his head.

"We had only brought enough food for three months, so it ran out. Trungpa and I cooked our yak leather shoes and bags for whatever nourishment they contained. When you're that hungry, there's no such thing as horrible.

"We started off with three hundred people, but many died en route, mostly of hunger. Sometimes we lost as many as twenty to thirty a day. It was winter and there were no berries or leaves, and we didn't know which were edible anyway. Things became more desperate when one of our party stole a cow for us all to eat, and the villagers told the Chinese about us. Troops descended on us, shooting, killing, and capturing those who didn't get away. When we reached the Brahmaputra, those of us that were left built coracles to cross the river. We crammed nine people into each boat, which was really treacherous, especially as we had to cross at night. The water came up to our mouths, and our clothing became wet and frozen.

"When Trungpa and I reached the other side, it was light and the Chinese were still chasing us. They were closing in fast and we could hear them coming. We were desperate for somewhere to hide, but there wasn't anywhere. Then we saw a large fallen tree with space underneath it. We crawled underneath and hid. The troops went over the tree three or four times, but didn't see us. We were very lucky. The following night we found a cave and crawled in there to sleep. We couldn't go any farther. There was no more leather to eat, and we were unable to walk anymore. Trungpa and I talked about which one of us was going to die first. I wasn't afraid—I had my meditation practice.

"We were still wearing precious relics and jewelry. I realized then we were decorated with useless things. At that moment, near death, I decided that if I managed to survive, the only job I would like to do is help others—education, clothing, medicine, food, shelter were the things that mattered. Everyone dies, whether they are rich or poor, have jewelry or not, but food and health are essential to all. I had been sitting on my throne all my life, giving orders, not being allowed into the kitchen of my monastery in case I got dirty. In that cave my mind changed completely. From then on I wanted to serve.

"By chance some hunters found us the next day and gave us food. What we hadn't realized was that we had already crossed the border and were safe. Out of the three hundred who had left Tibet, only fifteen of us made it to India."

Without much hesitation Freda invited them both to Delhi so that they could learn English. Chögyam Trungpa and Akong eventually moved into the already crowded Bedi government flat at Defense Colony and were absorbed into the family, as were most visitors. Once again Freda saw herself as mother and from then on referred to Trungpa as "my spiritual son."

"And I saw her as my mother," said Akong. "Who is the mother but the one who gives you nourishment, who takes care of you, who teaches you not to go near danger, who lets you grow to be a proper, useful human being? Without the mother the child could not survive. Freda Bedi was a real mother and very precious to me.

"Both Mummy and Papa Bedi were very kind. Whatever they ate they shared with us. I was not as keen to learn English as Trungpa— who was much better than me. Mummy Bedi was always busy, working hard every day, but she taught us whenever she could and would always take us along to parties at the embassies to introduce us to that kind of society so that we could get to know and understand it. She also wanted them to get to know Tibetans!" he said.

But it was not so easy for the Bedi children to have these new additions to their family. "They were with us for at least two years," Kabir recalls. "I was at college by this stage and Guli was at school, and they were there when we came home for the holidays. Initially I resented them a lot. To me they were interlopers. I hardly got to see enough of Mummy as it was. I really didn't like them being in our home at all. We hardly had any room. Just two bedrooms, a sitting room, and a hut that Papa had built in the garden, which functioned as an office. Guli and I slept with Mummy in one room, Trungpa and Akong shared the other.

"Then I grew to like them. They were very, very nice. Trungpa was extremely quick, flamboyant, with a naughty sense of humor. He took me under his wing. And you could not help liking Akong— he was humble, self-effacing, helpful. He was more solid and conservative than Trungpa. We remained close, and he referred to me always as his brother."

Guli was more resigned to the tulkus' presence in her home. "My life had always included other people—my mother was always bringing people into the house. She *did* care for her family, but we had to share her all our lives. It was part of the deal of being her child. I used to speak English with Trungpa and Akong, and I remember their day seemed extremely organized by Mummy. She made them keep to a timetable of when to get up, when to have their meals, when to have their lessons. My father, of course, was far less strict. He got Akong to take off his robes and wear ordinary shorts so that he could go to the market and have more fun."

Gelek Rinpoche was another frequent guest at the Bedi household. A highborn reincarnate lama related to the Thirteenth Dalai Lama, Gelek Rinpoche was found by Freda in the Buxa refugee camp, plucked out, and taught the niceties of how to behave in Western society, Professor Higgins–style. "I stayed with Mummy and her family on and off for about three years. Trungpa and Akong were already living with her. Trungpa was very diligent, but I was lazy. I felt I was on holiday! Mummy Bedi helped me get over my monk's superiority complex. She also taught me to respect women and other people in general.

"Her intention was to teach me about life outside my small monastic world. I was completely unaware of anything other than Tibetan life. She taught me to speak proper English. 'Don't run your words together, say them separately,' she'd instruct. Mummy would also take me to social events such as diplomatic parties. She would literally take me by the hand and show me how to enter a room, how to behave, and what to say. 'If you do not know the person, you put out your hand and say, slowly, "How do you do, how lovely to meet you."' Sometimes we acted out these scenes with her husband and two children, Kabir and Guli, as the audience.

"Mummy was very strict and stern, especially if I did not do my homework. But she was also very, very kind and extremely good at administration. Whatever she said she was going to do, she did it. She was completely generous with everything. Totally altruistic. There is no doubt she put me on the path for coming to the West. In fact, she told me to go to America. She said that Westerners needed the Dharma, that they needed help. She also told me that Westerners were more open than Tibetans and more forthright, which was encouraging. 'Whatever you know you can say—the more you say, the more they will understand. You don't have to hide.' She was correct," he said.

The small Delhi flat was now crammed to overflowing. Lois Lang-Sims, in *The Presence of Tibet*, summed up the flavor of the warm, eccentric, and chaotic Bedi household when she went to stay there while gathering information on the Tibetan refugee situation for the Tibet Society in London:

A tall, fair-haired Englishwoman with a face that was both soft and strong, looking remarkably Anglo Saxon despite the rumpled sari which she wore as if she had never known any other kind of dress, stood in the doorway of the ground floor flat to which I had found my way. She was smiling warmly in welcome. There seemed to be a great many people in the room in which I found myself, (including young monks, another fair-skinned woman in a sari and Freda Bedi's husband). They were all seated around a low table on the floor with the exception of an elderly Tibetan monk who was sitting apart from the rest on a raised seat.

The time was half past ten in the evening, but I could see the working day had only just finished. I began to look around the room which had a dingy beauty of its own. . . . There were no chairs, only cushions and mats, and the hard bed-seat covered by a Tibetan rug. In one corner of the room was a Tibetan shrine glowing with lighted butter lamps. As my eyes turned to the level of the ground, I saw a large brown rat sidling along the wall on soft feet.

At last I was shown the place where I was to sleep and the tap under which I was expected to wash. After a week in an Indian household I was still defeated by the sight of a cold tap splashing water onto a stone floor, a mug by which I realised I was expected to douche myself, nowhere to lay my clothes and no inch of floor space that was either dry or clean beneath my bare feet. The bed was of wood with no mattress; but at this I had become accustomed so that I even liked it. As a concession to my foreign habits I had been given a pair of sheets. I was sharing a room with an American woman while the other members of Freda's huge household disposed themselves to sleep either on the hard bed-seats or on the floor all over the rest of the flat. I was kept awake for most of the night by lights, snores, spiritual exercises, and campaigns against the bed bugs by the American.

The room in which I slept was used for meditation classes throughout the day and for part of the night so I could not enter it even to fetch a handkerchief. In Freda I had an example of an Englishwoman who had successfully Indianized herself, but I could not get behind the barrier of her total self-dedication, her all-pervading sense of social responsibility, her blind indifference to her comfort and convenience.

Scores of refugees came straggling down from the camps and appearing on Freda's doorstep, without money, food or decent clothes, and frequently in an advanced stage of sickness. Freda, being less concerned with categories than with individuals, never turned away a single Tibetan who came to her for help.

Trungpa was installed as the principal of the Young Lamas

Home School, and Akong was its manager. When all was complete, Freda had an audience with Nehru to thank him profusely for his help. Nehru smiled and said in a low, quiet voice, "It was not for *you* I did it." Nevertheless Freda had single-handedly planned and brought into being the Young Lamas Home School. She had succeeded in her pioneering task to bring the tulkus into the twentieth century, and she was on her way to realizing the next stage of her vision—to bring them to the West.

If Nehru provided the political clout for her school, the spiritual blessing was to come from the Sixteenth Gyalwa Karmapa, Freda's guru. She duly invited him to Delhi to perform the necessary rituals, and took advantage of his presence by requesting him to grant her Refuge, the formal ceremony marking one's official entrance onto the Buddhist path. Refuge confirmed Freda's faith that the Buddha, his teachings, and the community of his followers would provide her ultimate place of safety and succor, not just in this life but in all her lives to come. She was fifty, old for someone to take this step, but then she had been busy doing other things.

To Freda this was a hugely sacred and profound milestone in her spiritual journey. "When you take Refuge, you go on with your life, but in the cave of your heart you feel you have found the oasis, the place where you can take refuge in the sea of suffering, and where you can develop the enlightened mind. Taking Refuge is a great source of strength and blessing. Sometimes it can change your life, just like that. I've seen an unhappy life transformed almost immediately from taking Refuge," she said.

"Ultimately, in the Buddhist sense, Refuge is something within. We take Refuge in the seed of buddhahood, which is in all sentient beings. We think, 'May I aspire to that which is perfect within me and which already exists although I cannot see it. I want to remove the veils, not because the ego "I" wants it but so that I may help all beings.' We need a living guru, and we train to see the Buddha in him. That gives us the water to make the seed of enlightenment grow. Taking Refuge with His Holiness the Karmapa started my deeper meditation," she confided.

The duties of running her school were now added to her

considerable workload. Freda did not complain. "I now have seventeen young Tibetan reincarnate lamas in my latest effort for the refugees—such a joy to have them, and to see their happiness reflected in their faces," she wrote to Olive in her Christmas letter of 1961.

The pull of the Tibetans and her Buddhist practice were growing ever stronger, and the ties to her secular and domestic life weaker. Freda was in transition, on a halfway bridge between two worlds.

12

Dalhousie

THE INNER TENSION created by the pull between her secular and spiritual life could not last. By 1961 Freda had already
swapped her saris for long maroon dresses reminiscent of the robes
worn by Tibetan monks and nuns, although she still wore her hair
tied back in a bun. In the same year she quit her job at the Social
Welfare Board and moved the Young Lamas Home School and
herself from Delhi to Dalhousie, a former British hill station, in
the northern state of Himachal Pradesh, some 370 miles (595 kms)
from her flat and her family. Her commitment to the Tibetans and
her spiritual life was now almost complete.

Dalhousie was a beautiful town, spread over five hills, covered
in pine trees and inhabited by gangs of raucous monkeys and thousands of Tibetan refugees, who had been sent there by Nehru.
Formerly, it had been established as a hill station by Lord Dalhousie, former viceroy of India in 1854, and by the time Freda and her
young reincarnated pupils got there, it was full of decaying officers'
clubs, Anglican churches, and large English-styled houses with gardens full of roses and dahlias—all relics of the Raj. At seven thousand feet, it offered blessed relief from the searing sun of the plains
below, as well as breathtaking views of the Himalayas. An added
bonus was that another hill station, Dharamsala, a six-hour bus
journey to the south, was where the Dalai Lama had established his
base and government in exile.

Freda promptly rented a bungalow for herself and a large, imposing, once-magnificent two-storied brick British house, complete
with iron gates, for the new Young Lamas Home School. It had
many rooms, a large garden, and was perched on the edge of a hill.

Surrounded by the Tibetans and her tulkus, Freda felt contented and fulfilled. "Dalhousie air is crisp and fresh as new pine needles. To work for the lamas is blessing unlimited. I am happy here," she wrote to Olive.

If Freda was content, her family certainly was not. Over the years they had become accustomed to her frequent absences, and her children had developed a particularly strong sense of self-sufficiency and independence. Freda's new decision to move to Dalhousie, however, had particularly radical consequences.

"The problem was that by giving up her job she was giving up the family flat, as well as the small government salary that she was bringing in," said Kabir. "Life was hard enough as it was. Mummy was the principal breadwinner (and even her salary was low). Prices were rising, and there were school fees to be paid. Ranga was married, but Guli was only fourteen and was losing the only home she had. Where would she go on the holidays? Also, who was going to pay for my education? I was sixteen and about to enter St. Stephen's College, one of the best secondary schools in Delhi."

He complained bitterly, but Freda's response was cool, and practical. "Mummy sat me down and said frankly, 'I'm entering the religious path now and don't know how to support you.' She suggested I go and talk to the maharaja of Sikkim to ask if he could help. I went, was put up in a beautiful guesthouse, and addressed him politely: 'Sir I need some help with college fees.' 'Of course, how much do you need,' the maharaja replied. 'Twenty thousand rupees,' I said. He laughed. 'Are you sure that's enough?' he said. I wished I'd asked for more. He'd met Mummy when she'd been at the Karmapa's monastery in Sikkim and knew of her work—he respected her greatly." Freda's tireless work for others paid off in kind, if not in personal wealth.

Freda also offered to transfer Guli to the Sacred Heart Convent High School in Dalhousie so that she could be near her mother, but the independent-minded Guli opted to stay where she was. In the end Ranga and his wife, Umi, opened their home in Assam to both Guli and Kabir whenever they wanted it.

As for Freda's husband, BPL was making his own arrangements.

Their once-passionate love affair that had defied racial taboos had waned. The great goal that had united them in the very beginning and that glued them together during the dramatic early years of their marriage—the quest for Indian independence—had been achieved, and they both were now forging separate paths. In 1953, after her enlightenment experience in Burma, Freda had taken a vow of celibacy, the Brahmacharya Vow, whereas BPL had never been short of female admirers and had had many affairs.

"My father loved my mother, but he was a rake," said Guli. Women were drawn to him—he was a magnet, they would fawn all over him. He could *not* be monogamous. I remember him turning up at school with an Italian woman whom he introduced as a 'friend' but then drove off with her for a week, touring the mountains. I don't ever remember there being any cross words about his affairs at home, but my mother was under a lot of stress."

One particular liaison, however, caused serious tension in the family. When BPL's brother, the judge, died, he asked BPL to take care of his mistress, who was well known to Freda and the children as Auntie Raj. They would visit her from time to time and were on friendly terms. BPL took his brother's request seriously—and moved in with Auntie Raj and her daughter (who, the family insist, was not BPL's). "My mother never said it, but it broke her heart," said Guli. "My father adored my mother and always declared she was the love of his life. But he needed more."

No one truly knows why Freda made the serious decision to physically abandon her family and move to Dalhousie, but BPL's affairs may have made her choice easier. She certainly never expressed any ill feeling toward her husband, and in time stated she was even grateful to Auntie Raj for looking after BPL in his old age, when he was suffering from gout and a bad back. Freda and BPL remained on excellent terms throughout the rest of their separate lives, visiting each other when possible, keeping in constant touch about family matters and their respective activities. Freda's letters from all over the world invariably took on a respectful, even loving tone, addressing her husband as "My Dear Respected Babaji" (the title of the guru that he had become).

Freda was now free to concentrate on reestablishing the Young Lamas Home School in Dalhousie. With the Dalai Lama's permission, she put her spiritual son, Chögyam Trungpa, in charge of Spiritual Studies, and when he left, another eminent tulku, Ato Rinpoche (Dilgo Khyentse's nephew), took over. The school had about thirty pupils at any one time.

Freda, who was utterly nonsectarian in all religious paths, encouraged her pupils to stay true to their respective traditions, but she did want to introduce them to the formal studies of Geography, History, and the English language, through which, she envisioned, they would transmit the Buddha's message to the outside world. Certainly most of the young tulkus were not particularly interested in taking on such foreign subjects, and they approached their lessons in a somewhat desultory fashion. But Freda persisted.

In Dalhousie a colorful band of Westerners also encountered Freda (including the Beat poet Allen Ginsberg) as they made their way to the Young Lamas Home School to volunteer their services. Their impressions of the middle-aged Englishwoman provided unbiased, fresh insights into Freda the woman, because they were not dazzled by her fame, status, or supposed spiritual reputation.

When Diane Perry, a twenty-year-old from the East End of London, wanted to find a Tibetan guru, she wrote to Freda for help and was immediately summoned to the Young Lamas Home School. She was later ordained as Tenzin Palmo, and became well known for spending twelve years in retreat in the Himalayas, as told in my book *Cave in the Snow.*

Tenzin Palmo recalls, "It was March 1963 when I arrived in Dalhousie, having trudged the last two hours through snow. I found Mrs. Bedi in the kitchen standing over a stove that was gushing out smoke with no heat coming from it all. She was cooking porridge made with some Tibetan cheese. It was disgusting. She was a tall, plump woman in her midfifties, with blue eyes, an aquiline nose, and gray hair pulled back in a bun. I remember she was wearing a long maroon sari made of heavy woollen cloth, which made her look enormous. I was almost twenty-one and she was in her fifties, so there was a big age gap.

"She was a strong character—a strange mixture of Indian and English country. She never completely shed her roots. She was used to giving orders, and would not kowtow to anyone. She was great fun, full of confidence, and I admired and loved her very much.

"The thing was, she was very good at initiating ideas and getting money. At that time Tibetans were not yet organized, did not know English nor anything about aid agencies or how to find help. Freda Bedi, on the other hand, was extremely organized and excellent at presenting her case. Although she was superb at organizing others, Mummy wasn't very organized herself. Her room was always in a muddle—she could never find anything. She didn't have much money sense either. Quite a lot of money came in, and it all disappeared on small things, like sheets and towels. She could have bought property, which was very cheap then, and got herself established.

"The Tibetans were in awe of her, and were always going to her for help. She'd help everyone. She didn't care if they were lay, monastic, high, low, male, female, or what school of Buddhism they belonged to. Tibetans are generally quite narrow, keeping to their own sect, and Mummy, who treated them all the same, was an eye-opener to them. They were helpless and she was there. She saw herself as a mother, a universal mother, nurturing and wanting to reach out to help everyone. She saw a situation that was fraught and traumatic and in she stepped."

Another woman who experienced Freda's ability to break down barriers to get what she wanted was Joanna Macy, renowned American environmentalist, teacher, and author. She was living in Delhi with her husband, who was working for the Peace Corps, when Freda came to visit.

"I remember I opened the door and she stood there in her maroon clothes, greeting me as if somehow I and not she were the guest. I loved the way that touch of the Raj blended so paradoxically and superbly with the monk's garb she wore. She had come because she wanted my husband to release a particular person in the Peace Corps to work for her in Dalhousie. 'I shall speak to my friend Mr. B in the Cabinet,' Mummy said with a smile. 'When do you think we can expect him?' It was the marriage of serenity and sheer nerve. She was English in the way only the English can be. She had implicit authority," Macy said.

Later, Macy went to Dalhousie to help settle Khamtrul Rinpoche, a high lama who had escaped from Tibet with a huge number of followers, including monks and a large community of accomplished artists and craftspeople. She took the opportunity to take teachings from Freda at a small class for Westerners she had organized in Dalhousie. Macy also undertook a silent retreat under Freda's direction, and today acknowledges Freda's influence on her spiritual life.

"What she had to say had a lucidity and simplicity about it. I can't accept any teachings if there is a false note—if it is not coming from a person's wholeness and integrity, if what they are saying merely comes from what has been heard or read. With Freda I was able to drink it in. It was coming from beyond.

"I don't know how realized she was. I didn't go into those areas. She told me something about her mystical experience in Burma. She said she came out onto the street and saw everything in the world lit up as though from within. She did not go into a featureless expanse—but the ordinary world was transformed for her.

"She also taught me from her actions. I never heard her say a mean thing about anyone. She was *always* thinking of others, writing to people *all* the time, trying to get others what they needed. And it was done with such affection. She constantly had a folder in her lap, and whenever she had a minute, she'd write a note to someone.

"Mummy was wonderful for me to a very high degree," Macy continued. "First of all, she was important because she was a woman. I am grateful to someone who understood the teachings and practice, and that it was a woman in a tradition that is quite male dominated. That was not by choice—it was sheer good luck. I was not consciously being a feminist, but I knew and I trusted her. She had a love of the Dharma and used it in a bold, brave way. When I first approached her for teachings, she replied, 'Yes of course, my dear. I will be delighted. That is just the thing.' I sensed she had just been waiting for me to ask.

"Although she had reverence for the tradition, she did not present me with any overlay of doctrine or view. Nor did she start me off as the lamas would have done, with the Vajrayana (the Buddhism exclusive to Tibet). Instead, she wanted me to recapitulate her own journey, starting with the Theravada Buddhism she had learned in Rangoon. For me this was quite marvelous. It acquainted me with the early teachings of the Buddha and disciplined my mind in a way of following empirically my own experience in the immediate arising of mental and physical phenomena in my own body and mind. 'Bare attention—just watch the thoughts. Know you are thinking, thinking. Get the "I" out of it,' Mummy instructed. This allowed me later on in graduate school to approach the early teachings without any filter, with tremendous respect and curiosity for what the Buddha was saying. During my retreat I was in torment yet fascinated watching my own mind.

"She was trying to bring me right up to Tibetan practice. She kept talking about Trungpa, whom she loved very much. 'Wait till you meet him,' she said. When Trungpa came to the States, I thought, 'Now I'll graduate to a Tibetan practice,' but I stayed with the Vipassana I'd learned from Mummy.

"What Mummy did *not* do for me, however, was to model the social significance of the Buddha's teachings for our times, which is what I had become very focused on. 'Engaged Buddhism,' as it's called. To me Buddhism frees us to act for social and ecological survival, what needs to be done for a just and sustainable society. This wasn't of interest to Mummy."

Another volunteer was Faith Grahame, a wisp of a girl from Brighton, England, who ended up as Freda's secretary and then became a nun. Like Tenzin Palmo she had discovered an inexplicable calling to Tibetan Buddhism and found Freda Bedi through the Tibet Society, in Eccleston Square, London.

"I wrote to her. She said, 'Come! Come!' I was ready to board the ship for Mumbai, when all these boxes arrived on my doorstep.

They were full of books and food that Freda had procured from her many contacts in England, and she expected me to carry them along with my own luggage. There was no warning, no note saying, 'Do you mind?' That was Freda.

"I made my way up to Dalhousie and was met by this large woman with big, staring eyes, and a very loud voice that was bellowing orders at Indians. I was twenty, innocent and terrified! Over the next few years I got to know her better.

"She was a mixture of kindness, warm-heartedness, fearlessness, bossiness, and sensitivity. For example, I remember there was a nun whose left hand was going numb. Freda wrote a letter for her to take to the doctor, which I typed, wording the problem in technical language so that the nun would not be alarmed. In fact she had leprosy.

"She combined idealism, absolutely impracticality, and naïveté. For instance, she had this agent, a Sikh, who dealt with all the school's finances, whom she listened to like mad. Everyone knew he was swindling her, siphoning off funds to his family. He took a lot of money. But she would never believe it, both because he was a Sikh and because she only wanted to see the good in everybody."

One of Freda's ill-fated enterprises that Faith recalled concerned a buffalo that Freda decided to buy for some monks she was supporting at Andretta, a delightful artists' colony in the lush, picturesque Kangra Valley, Himachal Pradesh, where Freda had also built a small mud-brick house. "The trouble was the monks really didn't want this animal. They had to learn how to milk it, and looking after it took up a lot of time. One of the monks was very old. Nobody could understand what Mummy was thinking of," said Faith. In the end Ranga once again saved the day by taking the buffalo off the monks' hands.

While most of the young volunteers were frankly terrified of Freda's sometime-bossy, imperious manner, Alethea Ato was not. A bishop's daughter and fellow Oxford graduate, she was more than capable of holding her ground, even though she was thirty years younger than Freda. In 1965, Alethea had gone to India to help the Tibetan refugees. "I heard about Freda through a friend of a friend in Delhi. 'Freda has gone potty about Tibetans, but if you want to teach, she's the person to help you. Freda Bedi knows everybody.' It was true," recounted Alethea from her Cambridge, England, home where she lives with her daughter and husband, Ato Rinpoche, the handsome tulku she met and fell in love with at the Young Lamas Home School.

"She was a great 'caretaker of souls' and wanted to be mother to all the world. It didn't work with me. Freda was *not* my mother. Freda longed to instruct and was instrumental in getting certain texts translated into English. She was also big on faith and devotion, but I hadn't arrived in India to change my religion. Nevertheless she was an excellent teacher and I'm indebted to her for the lessons she taught me in Buddhism, which I've never forgotten.

"I admired her for her enterprise, no doubt about it. She had excellent contacts within the higher echelons of the Indian government. Once, when someone needed a visa, she swept into the consulate saying, 'I wish to see the high commissioner,' whom she knew personally. It was soon taken care of. She was also a marvel on Indian railways and commandeering cycle rickshaws.

"She could also do disastrous things. I remember she got a school in Yorkshire to raise money for a buffalo, and when they did, she wrote and said she was spending the money on hot-water bottles instead, because it was so cold. The school was horrified, replying they felt they'd raised the money under false pretenses."

Freda was definitely not pleased when Alethea, her valuable young English teacher, became romantically involved with Ato Rinpoche, who was an eminent lama, a nephew of the renowned Dilgo Khyenste Rinpoche, and recognized as the eighth incarnation of the Tenzin Tulkus. The liaison caused a huge scandal and a major disruption for the Young Lamas Home School.

"It meant him disrobing—a serious loss of a useful young lama. By then the Karmapa had lost Trungpa and as well, and it was beginning to be thought that it was a bad idea for rinpoches to learn English! Freda had a dewy, romantic view of tulkus; she thought them pure spirits. Although she may not have liked my relationship with Ato, she was not vituperative in any way. When I told her, she asked if I really meant it. I said yes. There were no rows, but I am sure it was a shock and disappointment to her. Once she knew I was sincere, she totally accepted it. We got married soon after in Delhi in February 1967. I was twenty-six.

"Ato had to tell His Holiness the Dalai Lama. He had an interview. We all waited with bated breath to see how the Dalai Lama would react—but the fact that the meeting lasted well over an hour was a sign that their relationship had survived."

In 1967, Alethea and Ato moved to Cambridge, England, had a daughter, and for years Ato worked as a nurse in a psychiatric hospital before starting to teach again in Europe and Canada. The next time Alethea saw Freda was in 1974, during one of the Karmapa's tours. "She was as charming and batty as ever. I suggested she might like to take a bath to freshen up when she arrived. 'I never take a bath after midday. The Karmapa advised me against it.' It was a harmless dottiness, but I felt sorry for those people who regarded every statement uttered by a lama as gold plated."

Ultimately, Alethea, like all those who encountered Freda and her work, had to concede her accomplishments. "One has to admit, however, that Freda made an awful lot happen. She saw very clearly what should happen, that the Tibetans needed to learn about the rest of the world. And she had the zeal of a new convert to bring it off. She had great conviction, and she was right!"

Another source of volunteers came via the international network she had established in Delhi, the Tibetan Friendship Group, through which Freda roped in pen pals, sponsors, and helpers for her tulkus and Tibetan refugees in general.

One such volunteer, John Weir Hardy, a particularly well-connected young man (educated at Eton, England's most exclusive and expensive private school), wrote glowingly in a newsletter of his experience with Freda:

> I left England embittered, having lost faith in humanity. Business life was never my strong point. The Tibetans have cured me of my despondency and have taught me much. They gave me the necessary balance which one must find to go through

life and Mummy was able to show me how to benefit from combining the spiritual with the material. Every fleeting second is a world in itself, another facet of a complex people's way of life, another glimpse into a world which is far more cultured than I have ever met.

And so the progress. Eton is taking much interest in the work and is going to run a major appeal in the hopes of raising about one thousand pounds, most of which will go toward a jeep.

Freda's Tibetan Friendship Group newsletter was one way that she let the outside world know about the plight of Tibet and what had happened to its people as a result of the Chinese invasion. In her lifetime she wrote literally tens of thousands of letters, usually working late into the night, to societies and individuals seeking funds, goods, skills, clothes, expertise, and anything else that was needed. She used all her skills of persuasion and journalism, making each letter intensely personal to encourage total involvement and therefore willingness to give. Her approach was quintessentially Freda, emphasizing human interest over intellectual argument:

This is Yangchen (picture provided), a little novice girl of Tilokpur, the Mahayana Buddhist nunnery. She is the politest little girl we have. Good manners are a little-considered virtue these modern days, but how comfortable it is to have a pleasant little girl like this. SHE NEEDS A SPONSOR [sic] at $7 a month, or even $5 for food. Her younger sister, Jayong, aged 7–8, is very bright, a darling child.

About a refugee school in Varanasi that she had visited and taken under her wing, she wrote,

There was a great deal of student poverty. They have scholarships, which are meager, but there are always emergencies—clothes to be bought and medicines beyond what can be provided. I wish someone could remember the students at Christmas. The boy that was helped with medicines (gift of Mrs. Mollie Noeltner, USA) still faces the operation and would need at least Rs 400 (about $54) for the heart drugs. Another student looks very TB-ish. Many of the pupils would love student pen friends. They would have to send postage money to the students, though. Even if no great sums were sent, it would give them a sense of companionship and courage.

The tulkus were learning English and their lessons on the modern world with varying degrees of success. Freda's star student, Trungpa Rinpoche, however, was making exceptional progress, and Freda's aspirations for him became increasingly ambitious. He had a natural aptitude for English and had taken to reading the poets that Freda presented him with, especially T. S. Eliot. He was keen on history and geography too. Freda decided that he was ready to try to get into Oxford, her own university, where he would receive the finest education the West had to offer. With such credentials he would be perfectly equipped and have the clout to bring the sacred Buddhist teachings to the outside world in a language it could understand.

With the help of John Driver, and Englishman who was also tutoring Trungpa, Freda set about getting a Spalding Scholarship for Trungpa, and succeeded. In early 1963 Trungpa set sail for England accompanied by Akong Rinpoche, to enter into the arcane, privileged, and hallowed halls of Oxford University. It was another epic journey into the unknown, heralding as many adventures, pitfalls, and triumphs as they had met in their escape from Tibet.

For both of them it was a tough entry into a strange world. Following his desire to become a doctor, Akong broadened his knowledge of Western medicine by working as an orderly at Churchill Hospital. It was a rude awakening.

"If I hadn't had the Buddhist teachings and some understanding of the mind, I would have hanged myself," he confessed. "It's quite hard being on a throne one day and cleaning toilets another. Eventually I got to like my work and now I am very grateful for the experience. And the wages helped support Trungpa and myself. I was never any good at study. I was only interested in helping people. In the end I was allowed into the operating theater to watch. I enjoyed that. I learned a lot. I was rather sad that I had to give it up when we moved to Scotland," he said, referring to their establishing of Samye Ling in 1967, the first Tibetan monastery in the West, in the small town of Eskdalemuir.

As for Trungpa, apart from an excellent education, he acquired a British passport, an Oxford accent, a predilection for dining in formal settings with fine china and candlesticks, beautifully tailored suits, and a liking for English protocol and manners. He put it all to good use in his innovative ministry when he moved to the United States in 1970, accompanied by his very young English bride, Diana Pybus.

13

The Nuns

IT WAS NOT ONLY the bright young tulkus whom Freda was busily gathering up. A handful of nuns were also roaming around the Dalhousie hills, lost and forsaken. Of the 200,000 nuns that had existed in Tibet, only 156 had managed to escape, and they were scattered around various refugee settlements in India with no one to organize or help them.

Their fate was the result of their fiercely patriarchal culture that had always favored the monks' education and welfare over that of the nuns. The monks had had their mighty, rich, and powerful monasteries, fertile seedbeds of spiritual learning and practice, with brilliantly organized infrastructures. The nuns, on the other hand, had been relegated to small, poor dwellings, and were generally regarded as second-class citizens due to their novice ordination. Consequently, while the monks were educated in the profound scriptures in which Tibetan Buddhism excelled and were taught sacred art and dance and the skill of debate, the nuns were reduced to saying simple prayers and rituals, or serving the monks in the monastery kitchen.

In spite of their reduced status, however, the nuns had proved themselves every bit as sincere, feisty, high-spirited, and enormously brave in their religious devotion as the monks. During the brutal Chinese invasion and destruction of their country's unique spiritual heritage, the nuns, young and old, armed with nothing but their courage, repeatedly marched on their oppressors. Shaking their fists and, shouting "Long live the Dalai Lama!" many were thrown into jail, horribly tortured, killed, and starved for years on end.

As for their spiritual capacity, Tibet had produced some of the mightiest women meditators of all, the yoginis, who went it alone, living for years in remote, high Himalayan caves, not shaving their heads but letting their hair grow long and wild and reemerging so bright that even the male yogis acknowledged their superior attainments.

Always a champion of women, Freda took one look at the few Dalhousie nuns and was moved to help them. Further up the hill from the Young Lamas Home School she found an abandoned villa that once belonged to a British sahib, with a glassed-in veranda and an overgrown garden. It would do splendidly, she thought, and promptly moved the nuns in. She called it the Nun's Hermitage and immediately set about writing innumerable letters to her vast international network of supporters, seeking funds for robes, food, medicine, and material necessities "to support these nuns in their life of higher meditation and service to mankind." It was yet another project to manage in her already overflowing self-appointed portfolio, and one that was especially close to her heart.

Well-schooled by Barbara Castle in equality for women during her Oxford days, Freda had big plans for her nuns. Her vision was to build them a permanent nunnery, a separate retreat center, and then an institute for the higher studies that had been denied them for centuries. Such an education would put them on a par with the monks. She understood that saying prayers and doing rituals were not sufficient to reach the highest goal of Buddhism, the realization of ultimate reality that, along with a heart filled with compassion for all sentient beings, brought one to enlightenment. For that, one first needed fluency in extensive philosophical teachings until one grasped the meaning intellectually, and then one had to meditate on one's understanding until it became a lasting "realization," embodied as a known reality, having dropped from the head into the heart.

The year was 1963, and such an idea was monumentally radical. Today there is a thriving movement to bring equality to Tibetan nuns, but back then no one had ever thought of giving women such a treasure. No one thought that women could be enlightened. After all, the word *woman* in Tibetan translated as "inferior born." A woman's body was deemed simply unfit to contain the splendor of full awakening, a privilege belonging exclusively to the male. Freda was having none of it. She was decades ahead of her time.

Wasting no time, she found a piece of land near a river in Tilokpur, a small village sixty-two miles from Dalhousie and about twenty-two miles from Dharamsala, home of the Dalai Lama and his newly formed government in exile. To Freda's mind it was Buddha-sent. Not only was it peaceful but it was near a cave once occupied by Tilopa (988–1069 C.E.), a renowned Indian mystic, erudite scholar, monk, and Tantric practitioner who founded the Kagyu lineage, of which her guru, the Karmapa, was now the head. Freda could not have been more excited.

Her letter to the Karmapa requesting permission to build her nunnery rang with confidence, and also revealed the extent of the success she had already achieved: "At the time of moving from Dalhousie, the nunnery has collected together and trained in Dharma, handicrafts, and languages, forty nuns of all ages, keeping the tradition of the Tibetan nuns going and giving them confidence to face the future. Twenty-five postulants are also waiting for admission."

With the Karmapa's approval, Freda began to build. It was not a success. In spite of her dewy-eyed vision, the site turned out to be utterly unsuitable. Faith Grahame, the English girl who had become her secretary, recalled the disaster in these words: "Being on a sand bank by a river, it was full of mosquitoes. It was also as hot as hell there, and right next door to a school, which made it extremely noisy. There was no water and the nuns had to walk miles in the heat to collect it. It was also full of monkeys, who would attack and steal anything the nuns would put outside. But Freda was sold because Tilopa had meditated there. That was her idealism. She was totally impractical."

The problem was solved when the grass huts that Freda and the nuns were living in while they built the nunnery caught fire, and were razed to the ground, destroying their belongings and many precious texts that Freda was in the midst of translating.

Undeterred, Freda found another, infinitely more suitable site on a hillside overlooking the original piece of land, and began building afresh. It was a mammoth, exhausting, even noble endeavor, as was obvious from a letter she wrote to Sheila Fugard, poet and devoted South African student, wife of the renowned South African playwright Athol Fugard.

"Our nunnery is something of an odyssey," she wrote. "We are clearing bricks and mud from the floor of a ruined fort on top of the hill. It seems like a mountain. We are using Tibetan and Indian labor, as well as nuns of all sizes, including me carrying stones for an hour a day. Our little nuns carry pebbles."

What she did not mention was that there was no road to the new site, which involved Freda and the nuns having to haul the rocks and stones up the steep hillside by hand, often in the blazing Indian summer heat. Freda, now fifty-seven years old and heavier than she had been in her youth, was not the best equipped to handle hard labor. The nunnery, which comprised a *gompa* (temple), classrooms, sleeping quarters, and a kitchen, was finally completed in 1968. Twenty-seven nuns, under the watchful eye of Freda and an abbot, Lama Thinley Rinpoche, moved in. She called it Karma Drubgyu Thargay Ling and dedicated it to her guru, the Sixteenth Karmapa.

Freda had accomplished another first—building the first religious establishment for Tibetan refugee monastics of either gender. The girls had finally beaten the boys to it!

While the Young Lamas Home School for young tulkus was disbanded a few years after Freda opened it, her nunnery still exists to this day. You can find it perched high on its hill with beautiful views overlooking tree-clad slopes and within earshot of the river rushing past below. There's now a road leading to the nunnery, which boasts a fine pair of iron gates decorated with traditional Tibetan motifs. In the courtyard is a bodhi tree grown from a seed that Freda brought from Bodhgaya, a descendant of the very tree under which the Buddha sat pledging not to move until he attained enlightenment. The sapling was six inches high when she planted it, today it is enormous.

In the temple is a large Tibetan statue of the Buddha, which Freda also carried up the hillside, and next to it is a beautifully scripted manuscript in Freda's own handwriting. It reads, "You who are the very image of Shakyamuni, for the sake of all that lives completed your years in Tibet, the land of snows. Now you have come back to your home, the noble land of India. Remembering you within us raises happiness beyond all vision."

Beside the Buddha in a glass cabinet is a large photo of Freda in nun's attire, with eyes raised heavenward, signed "With blessings, Gelongma Mummy."

Although some of the original buildings are in serious need of repair, Freda's own small house remains standing, as a shrine to her memory. There is no doubt that she is revered by all sixty-five nuns who now live there.

"We all keep Mummy in our hearts," said Ani Wangchuk, one of the original Dalhousie nuns whom Freda took in. Just escaped from Tibet, she was in a perilous state, like the rest of her sisters, lacking money, provisions, a roof, or aid of any kind. "As nuns we did not know what to do, so we all went to her. We were very young and special to her. She would hold our hands and say, 'I will make new robes for you. Don't worry. I'll pay for everything.' She knew the future for us nuns. She knew everything. She bought all this land and built the nunnery, carrying rocks and cement up the hill. Mummy-la was so kind. She wanted this nunnery to be a special place to give the nuns a big education.

"We can't say for sure if she is Tara, but she is very special, because she knew Buddha in her heart. She lived with us for quite a long time and had many visitors. I wish she were still here. I miss her."

This was 2014 and among the Tibetans, if not the Westerners, Freda's name was still being linked with the female buddha, Tara.

Her ambitions also included a craft shop where they could raise money by selling embroidered panels, coffee, and doughnuts to tourists on the road below and, of course, the beloved buffalo! "A good buffalo and two high-milk-yielding cows are needed to fill our needs and sell milk to the village and local restaurant. It will make our diet more nutritious and give us some necessary cash income. Cost of cattle and shed, Rs 3,000."

It was another one of Freda's impractical schemes. No one was able to look after the buffalo, and as mentioned earlier, Ranga was summoned to transport the beast to his own home on the other side of the continent. The café-cum-craft shop also came to nothing.

The nunnery itself, however, was running well under the democratic structure that Freda imposed. She felt that the nunnery should be run by a committee of nuns who would administer and plan its development. This was a radical departure from tradition, in which nuns, and monks for that matter, unquestioningly obeyed a strict hierarchical structure. Freda, the socialist, was first and foremost for freedom, in religion as in every other avenue of life. Now, in the new millennium, other Tibetan nunneries are following Freda's blueprint, but in the 1960s, Freda was a trailblazer. "This is a very necessary development," said Frida. "I want them to be in charge of their own destinies and gain confidence in their own abilities. The *ani-las* will learn many things when they decide matters for themselves. They are good nuns and will, I am sure, be able to fulfill their responsibilities very well."

Just when Freda thought that all was settled and secure with her burgeoning nunnery, danger threatened to destroy everything that she had achieved. She learned that plans were being made to relocate the nuns to the new refugee settlement in South India. Like a tigress rearing to protect her nuns and her ambitions for them, she went straight to the top. In a brusque letter to the Dalai Lama himself, she underlined in no uncertain terms what had been accomplished and what she expected him to do.

Your Holiness,
My devotion at your sacred lotus feet.

Various matters concerning the Karma Drubgyu Thargay Ling Nunnery in Tilokpur HP have been brought to my notice, particularly the effort made to "rehabilitate" them to a Tibetan settlement in South India.

With the help of donors and friends I have been able to

build for the use of the Kagyu nuns of this and succeeding generations a complex of buildings dedicated to H. H. Gyalwa Karmapa:

1. A big stone shrine, 20 x 30 feet with polished cement floor.
2. An L-shaped building. Two stories with separate apartment units that can house the nuns, plus two small cell rooms. Communal kitchen, store, bathing-and-toilet units.
3. Three big rooms attached to the shrine for head nun and Protector Shrine chapel. A small building containing a room and kitchen store for myself. A dormitory plus kitchen for Tibeto-Frontier nuns.
4. Guest rooms, each with kitchen and veranda as a self-support scheme to help the nuns earn. Income comes from offerings, sponsors and friends. They are therefore settled and HAVE NO NEED TO BEG [sic].
5. I have plans to provide more bathrooms. (We have a miraculous spring that appeared on our land near the shrine after prayers to H. H. Karmapa.) I also envision a study course in Tibetan Medicine, medical care of aged and seriously sick nuns, and a Hermitage for retreat, along with its own land.

There is no reason, therefore, why any nun should be persuaded to settle in the South.

Faced with the force and fluency of Freda's words, the Dalai Lama recanted. The nuns were allowed to stay where they were.

Other problems, much closer to home, were bubbling not far below the surface—portents of a pending schism that surfaced after Freda died. Sad though it was, such conflicts were not unknown within the annals of Tibetan history, which abounded with tales of fierce rivalries between monasteries, where power, politics, and spirituality collided. Freda was well aware of what was going on in her nunnery.

"There have been some rather ugly undercurrents at the nunnery and I think there are outside political (Tibetan) influences brought to bear," she confessed to a friend, without elaborating on the specifics. "The nuns are not solely to blame. There are, in any case, two 'troublemakers' among them, and the young nuns are becoming increasingly conscious of the way they are being misled. I won't go into the whole sad story, as it doesn't help TFG (Tibetan Friendship Group) or the nuns, and we are only concerned with that, so we must bear all the misunderstandings and untruth and pray (for the younger group) that things clear up."

As Freda feared, a schism eventually happened. A second nunnery, called Drupten Pedme Gatsal Ling, was built on the plains below the original nunnery. An impressive building situated on three acres of land and boasting a large temple, solar heating, and other modern conveniences, it now houses forty-four nuns, with more expected. Whatever bad feeling exists between the two nunneries, the abbess, Karma Tsultrim, an imposing sixty-year-old with a no-nonsense manner, holds Freda in the highest esteem, and often carries her picture. "When I think of Mummy, I see her in meditation. She was always in the meditative state, even when she was not sitting on the cushion. We Tibetans think she was Tara, because she was so kind. Mummy-la was always soft, never angry. If the younger ones were naughty, her face would go strict but she would never shout," said Karma Tsultrim.

She justified her founding the rival nunnery this way: "I think Mummy would like there to be two nunneries. Why not? She supported the nuns' cause very much."

There were troubles on other fronts as well. Freda's health was beginning to falter. In 1970, she wrote to Olive of the recurrence of bronchial trouble, the illness that was to kill her seven years later, admitting how seriously ill she had been and speaking touchingly of the care her nuns and others had showed her. "You will hardly believe it, but I am convalescent after twenty-eight days' continuous fevers and bronchial flu. I was so ill, and I cannot tell you with what devotion the nuns have nursed me—and in fact how kind all the villagers have been. I am distinctly thinner and still weaker than my usual hearty self, but I'm so much better."

Of all her nuns, no one was more devoted than Pema Zangmo, a former cowherd from Kinnaur (on the Tibetan-Indian border) who became Freda's close, utterly dedicated personal assistant. She had met Freda in 1965 in Dalhousie when she was just twelve years old, having escaped from Kinnaur with her parents. All her life she had harbored a deep spiritual longing, and when Freda helped her take novice vows (with her parents' permission), Pema Zangmo's gratitude knew no bounds. Until Freda died, Pema Zangmo served and protected her with a rigor that bordered on the ferocious. A short, feisty, outspoken woman, she could boss everyone around, including Freda if she thought it were in her mentor's best interests. Freda called her a "jewel," but acknowledged that jewel could be a "rough diamond."

Today Pema Zangmo can be found tilling the soil and planting vegetables in a large, empty complex of buildings on the plain below the nunnery, which she hopes to fill with incumbents eager to begin Freda's vision of higher learning. With that in mind she teaches regularly in France, gathering support and finances. Still strong and remarkably feisty, her devotion to Freda and her admiration for who she was and what she accomplished has not waned at all. Pema Zangmo has no doubts that Freda was and remains an embodiment of Tara, the female Buddha of Compassion in Action.

"Mummy-la is a bodhisattva. She knew many things and everybody loved her. She and the Karmapa (her guru) were very close. Whatever he asked her to do, she obeyed. The Karmapa told me to look after her. He told me directly, 'She is an emanation of White Tara.' He also said that he and Mummy-la were of the same essence."

It was a remarkable statement. Pema Zangmo, as an eyewitness, was offering confirmation of the loudly whispered rumor, that Freda, an English family woman from Derby, was regarded by the eminent Sixteenth Karmapa as a manifestation of a female Buddhist deity, and hinted that she bore the same spiritual evolution as himself. Whether Freda herself accepted such an eminent status is not known, but she was certainly aware of the importance of White Tara (or Jetsun Dolkar, her Tibetan name) within the Buddhist faith, as she wrote to her Australian friend Joan Wilson, an avid Tibetan Friendship Group supporter.

"Jetsun Dolkar is the white form of our Divine Mother Bodhisattva. We think there is a Heavenly Mother to whom we can appeal when life's problems get too much. The White Tara makes us wise: That is the meaning of the four extra eyes on the palms of her hands and the one in the middle of her forehead. She is always peaceful, always pleasant and welcoming—see her open hand. We need mothers."

For the Tibetans, trained to see all beings as carrying the seed of potential buddhahood within, the leap to regard Freda's qualities as divine was not implausible. She had appeared at the hour of their need, was impartial about whom she helped, was kind and exceptionally able at getting things done. To them Freda, or Mummy-la, looked like Tara. For skeptical Westerners, however, the jump was not as easy. Not one of her European, American, or Australian friends and colleagues saw her as divine.

Nevertheless, amid the administration of both the Young Lamas Home School and the nunnery, the constant letter writing seeking funds, the organizing of papers for the ceaseless stream of refugees, and the finding of volunteers, Freda's own spiritual vocation was far from forgotten. It had begun in her childhood, blossomed in Burma, and brought her to this point of working for the Tibetans. It was, in fact, calling ever louder, beckoning her, in her late middle age, to an entirely new, infinitely larger, and more ambitious way of life.

14

Ordination

FREDA NOW FELT that she had bided her time long enough. For years she had been wearing long maroon dresses in the style of a Tibetan Buddhist nun, and ever since her enlightenment experience in Burma she had espoused celibacy as a way of life. "Celibacy heightens compassion, and the energy to transmit teachings. Sublimated sexuality is the means of this transmission," she said. She was already halfway there. Several times she had asked the Karmapa if she could be ordained. He had replied that she already had the ordination in spirit and that she needed to wait until he could confer it officially. In Freda's mind the only obstacle were her children. When she reached the age of fifty-five, she deemed the time was finally right. Kabir was twenty and Guli almost eighteen—old enough, Freda thought, for them to withstand the possible psychological blow taking robes might entail suggesting a possible severance from her family, deeper and stronger than the merely physical.

Conventionally, Freda's decision to remove herself emotionally, mentally, and physically from worldly concerns in order to commit herself totally to the religious life could be regarded as selfish and irresponsible. But Freda had always followed her heart, her deepest aspirations, and her destiny, regardless of what anyone thought. At another level her decision was merely the natural progression of the trajectory she had followed since childhood. Throughout her life, her spiritual calling was never far below the surface; it had informed both her political and her social work.

"Although I was engaged in political activity, I was never interested in politics. I'm interested in freedom. Freedom of the mind. And when I took up social work, as well as writing and teaching, the deep feeling was for freedom, integrity, and human dignity, which was accomplished by Mahatma Gandhi, who taught us the way of love. This is the Christian way too. When somebody wants to knock your head with a stick in a demonstration, you offer your head to be hit. You sit down. You don't run away. And you don't feel a minute's resentment against your adversary. Many of the Indian police were decent people who just wanted to make a living to care for their wives and kids.

"Of course, I was a political and social activist, but inwardly there was always meditation. I don't think I could have borne those years, with all the difficulties, all the strain if I had not done so. I think meditation should be integrated with home life from an early age. The earlier the better. I don't think the strains of the modern world can be borne unless you have an inner, meditative life. It leads to saner people, who don't crack up or have to go to mental hospitals or take sleeping tablets. These are all due to excessive strain," she said.

"The basis of a spiritual life, whether you are ordained or lay, is nonviolence. Not to harm others, otherwise you yourself will be harmed. The law of karma comes in. It's like throwing a pebble in a pool—the ripples of harming go far."

Freda's mind was made up. She had reached the point of no return.

She elaborated this feeling in a letter to her South African friend and disciple Sheila Fugard: "Transient pleasure had already fallen away—it was an urge to leave the Wheel of Existence. Enough of suffering. The facts of being born, bearing illness, growing old, and dying are painful. Even Prince Siddhartha (the Buddha) was forced to leave wealth and a wife and infant son. One must resolve the knot of existence—cut the roots of desire, examine one's life and see how one is bound to samsara.

"The warmth of love and compassion remained, however, but in a wider context. All sentient beings are deserving of compassion. All compounded things wear out. These problems require deep meditation. The path is never an easy one."

In her eyes the whole world had now become her family.

She completely misjudged, however, her family's reaction to her news. BPL reportedly wept. Kabir, who was still at college, was horrified.

"We had no money—I mean no money. And my mother was becoming a nun. I was devastated, and extremely angry. She was not going to be there for me, she had given herself to the Buddha. I felt utterly abandoned. I no longer had a mother. 'Why now?' I asked her. 'When does the apple fall from the tree?' she replied."

It was not just for himself that Kabir was worried. Always his little sister's champion, he was anxious about who would guide and protect Guli in the future, especially in the matter of choosing a husband. He wrote his fears to Freda. Her response was immediate, heartfelt, eloquent, and some would say naive. In her mind the trust she was about to put in the Buddha by becoming a nun would automatically safeguard her children by throwing a blanket of holy protection around them. Karma would guide the way, and her love for them was undying.

"Your letter of the twenty-ninth reached me yesterday. I am sending off a telegram today and this letter. Since yesterday I have been in a maze of pain, feeling yours and Guli's. I thought that, with the special understanding we all have for one another, the birth could be painless. But I had not realized the cutting of the birth cord must cause pain. It heals. The link between the baby and the mother does not cease. It continues. Nothing ceases. In a way this time I am the baby. And I need you all, your love and protection.

"Basically it's Guli that you are thinking of. The feeling for a daughter is more protective. . . . Guli is deep inside me, in an inner way. She knows it. In her childhood I gave her all the protection I could; now I am giving it to her in a higher way. But she is always with me. The question of her marriage has been in my mind. This winter in Calcutta I asked for H. H. Karmapa's prediction (infallible). He said, 'After finishing her studies, she will find a good home.' That reassured me on the physical plane.

"Kabir, I don't think Guli need worry for a good three or four years more about this. Let her study peacefully. These days the old 'arranged' marriages are not so usual in families like ours. Ranga and Binder 'arranged' their own, and dowries were not the question. Karma plays a big part. Possibly Guli will meet someone in our circle of friends who likes Papa and me anyway.

"You know—I have shown it in so many ways and it is invisibly always there, that there is a special link between us. A trust. Here, too, there has been complete trust. You all knew one day this step would be taken; we even joked about my losing my hair! Somehow, now had to be the time. The inner renunciation was complete long ago. . . .

"I can't write about things so deep inside they are beyond words. Speaking is a little easier (I told Papa), but paper does not really convey the necessity—not just for me but for all of you too. But I did feel—still feel—that you would understand.

"Something has happened inside me. To take an ordination in direct line from the Buddha is an inexpressibly sacred thing. In a way an ordination is not only a renunciation: It is a protection, a way. Again, don't ask me to put into words what cannot be put into words. There is an inner time, a ripeness, a realization of the impermanence of life, of suffering, of others, not only of oneself. A reflection of the great compassion of the Buddha. At that time the knowledge of the approaching birth comes.

"Things are the same, at least outwardly, except for my dress. We will meet and spend holidays together as usual. Mother love doesn't just dry up. I can still see your little face as it was when you drank my milk, and Guli on her first birthday with that full-moon face of hers. You needed me then; you need me now. I am still there. If Papa at anytime needs me in advancing age I am also still there. There's so much more I want to say, but I can't write more. Except to say you are both near, like the blood in my veins. With love, Mummy."

Freda never told Guli what she was planning. Just as she had deposited her in boarding school at age five without any prior warning, astonishingly she never discussed with her teenage daughter her intention to become a nun. Once again, Guli was presented with a fait accompli. Freda's behavior was baffling. Was it guilt? Fear of Guli's reaction? Whatever Freda's reason, Guli was emotionally winded.

"I remember exactly how I found out," Guli said. "Kabir was renting a place in Delhi and I went to see him. He casually dropped into the conversation that our mother had become a nun. 'We won't ever have to buy her a comb again,' he joked, trying to make light of the situation. I was *not* happy. Somewhere inside me I felt sad. I thought she wouldn't be there for me and that she could have waited until I was settled with a husband and home of my own. At another level I wasn't surprised at what she had done—she had been wearing maroon saris for ages. But I felt she should have told me herself.

"Admittedly, I was a difficult teenager! I used to get really mad at her. Once, when she wouldn't allow me to go to a dance, I refused to go home in the holidays and went to stay with Ranga and Umi instead. I think Mummy felt there would be less turmoil about being ordained if she told me after the fact," she said.

On August 1, 1966, Freda was ordained as a Buddhist nun by the Karmapa in his newly built monastery at Rumtek Monastery, in Sikkim. It was a huge, magnificent building, constructed in traditional Tibetan style, rising in tiers up the mountainside. In its elaborately decorated temple, resplendent with intricate wood carvings, gold and scarlet paint, exquisite cloth paintings of deities, and vast statues of the Buddha, the Karmapa bestowed on Freda the new name of Karma Tsultrim Kechog Palmo, shortened to Sister Palmo.* Known as "The Going Forth," the ordination formalized entering into homelessness, the traditional state of the Buddhist monk or nun—ironically, a condition that Freda had already known for a several years.

As a novice nun (the only ordination allowed to Tibetan nuns), Freda's vows outnumbered those required of monks. At the basic level they included not to kill any living thing, steal, tell lies, or take intoxicants. She promised to remain chaste, eat moderately, and have no bank account. Finally, she donned the proper robes and shaved her head.

---

* Karma means "karma kagyu," Tsultrim "ethics" or "discipline," Kechog means "supreme knowledge" or "learning," and Palmo means "glorious lady" or "heroine." Put together it reads as: Glorious lady of the Karma Kagyu lineage upholding supreme knowledge and ethics.

"Losing your hair is an acid test. For a woman, whatever the age, it's very difficult to give up your hair unless it doesn't mean anything anymore. It's what keeps thousands from taking the vow," she admitted. Freda emerged bald, transformed, and extremely happy. "It's a *tremendous* step. It provides great strength because a whole stream of blessings of the lineage from Buddha to pupil to pupil down the ages comes like a vast stream, washing away the bad karmas and murky things that have been there," she explained.

Following her ordination Freda moved her base to Rumtek Monastery to be near the Karmapa. She was the only woman in the entire establishment, an extraordinary privilege. Her status was further enhanced by being given a room just below that of the Karmapa, who was installed at the highest point of the vast monastery complex, in keeping with Tibetan tradition. It was a great honor, indicative of the high esteem in which she was held. In contrast to the bright splendor of Rumtek's exterior, however, Freda's room was small and modest, containing a bed, which coupled as a meditation seat; a small table; and a chair for visitors.

Freda's life in Rumtek took on a new rhythm. Sitting with the Karmapa every day, she became his right-hand woman, liaising between him and outside visitors, especially officials and government representatives, whom she was superbly experienced to deal with. She kept a firm, motherly eye on the four energetic young Regents who were poised to take over from the Karmapa when he died. And, in her own time, she wrote translations of Tibetan scriptures and prayers, oversaw her nunnery, and kept up a copious stream of correspondence to members of her Tibetan Friendship Group all over the world. Occasionally, she managed to slip into silent retreat, to advance her meditation practice and further her spiritual growth.

The Karmapa had bigger plans for his Western nun, however. Audaciously, he broke with entrenched, centuries-old, patriarchal Tibetan ecclesiastical tradition, which kept nuns on the lower rungs of the spiritual ladder, and urged Freda to travel to Hong Kong and take the higher *bikshuni* ordination available to Chinese Buddhist nuns. This would bestow on Freda status equal to that of a monk. It was a bold and gigantic step for the Karmapa to take. As a bikshuni, Freda would be allowed to receive all the teachings and initiations that lead to enlightenment.

The Karmapa knew that only a Western woman of Freda's reputation, ability, and education would have the confidence to take such a radical step, and more importantly, be listened to by the Chinese Buddhist authorities. The Karmapa was so committed that he wrote to the king of Bhutan asking him to fund Freda for the journey. The king complied.

To ensure his vision was turned into reality, the Karmapa traveled three times to Hong Kong to talk the matter over and lay the groundwork. In December 1971 Freda made the historic journey to take the full bikshuni ordination of the Mahayana line from the Buddhist Sangha Association headed by Venerable Minh Chi and Venerable Sek Sai Chung. She stopped off en route in Burma to pay her respects to the teachers who had put her on the path, and to seek their blessing for what she was about to do. "I always feel very close to my Burmese teachers," she said.

She found Burma poorer and sadder and the people less lighthearted under military rule. Sayadaw U Pandita, however, now an old man, had retained the same charming sense of humor. He asked after her family and gave her the quintessential Buddhist teachings: Cease to do evil, do what is good, and purify the heart. Freda replied that Tibet's favorite mantra, OM MANI PADME HUM ("Hail to the jewel in the lotus"), when fully understood, meant the same thing.

Landing in Hong Kong she was disappointed that no one was there to meet her. Always short of money and cost-conscious, she was horrified at the cost of the taxi to the Chinese Temple in the New Territories, where the bikshuni ordination was to take place. "Fifty HK dollars—that's about seventy rupees," she complained in a communication to her family.

When she arrived, she found three other women waiting to be ordained, together with the twenty priests required to perform the ceremony, a vast crowd of onlookers, and a television crew eager to record the first woman in 1,100 years to receive full ordination in the Tibetan tradition. Freda fasted and prayed and had her head freshly shaved down to her scalp. She put on the black robes of the Chinese order and took the Bodhisattva Vow again:

> However innumerable beings are, I vow to save them
> However inexhaustible the passions are, I vow to extinguish them
> However immeasurable the Dharmas are, I vow to master them
> However incomparable the Buddha truth, I vow to attain it.

The ceremony started at five o'clock in the morning and lasted for two days. Freda, now sixty years old, heavy, and not used to such physical exertion, found the whole thing exhausting.

"It was very strenuous and absolutely agonizing for my old knees. We were constantly bowing, up and down, walking, and kneeling—one was quite dizzy. I must have lost pounds. We didn't stop till midnight—with just half an hour's rest for a cup of tea," she said. "Tibetan Buddhism is more contemplative. We sit for hours in the lotus position—and do not move!"

The climax of the ordination was an extraordinary ritual dating back to the Song dynasty, designed to test the faith and commitment of the initiate: The aspirants burned the last joint of their little fingers as a demonstration of their willingness to surrender their bodies in the service of all humanity. This was how the Bodhisattva Vow was taken at that time. By Freda's time, the test had taken a new form: Small incense cones were placed on top of the aspirant's bald head, lit, and allowed to burn down to the scalp. The really hardy aspirant had nine, twenty-one, or one hundred and eight cones—all significant numbers in Buddhism.

"The abbot explained it was a voluntary offering to the Buddha," said Freda. "I thought to myself, 'I am here to take the ordination and if that's what's involved, I'll do it.' I felt that if I meditated right, I should not feel the burning. The ego in me said it would have been infinitely preferable if there were not so many people and press around, but they had great respect for the monks and nuns and it benefited them to watch, as it increased their faith. But still, it would have been better if we had been alone," she added wistfully.

"I grew very absorbed in the ceremony and began meditating strongly on the indivisibility of the Buddha and the Karmapa, who is very Buddha-like." Her concentration became so great that, she claimed, she did not feel the burn at all.

"How long it went on for, I do not know. No words can express the effect of the ceremony. There was an incredible feeling of lightness and light. When it was over, I was conscious of a little soreness, but I have to tell you I did not feel pain once. The scars only appeared back in Rumtek ten days later. Getting the ordination is not simply a matter of someone picking up a book and following the instructions. It has to be done by masters who hold the lineage. Since receiving it I have felt incredibly pure and enriched in every way," she declared.

Her return to Rumtek was jubilant. The entire monastic community together with the villagers turned out in force, waving banners and showering on her great heaps of *katags*, white ceremonial scarves to welcome and pay homage to the first bikshuni in the Tibetan tradition. Once again, Freda had become a pioneer. She was written up in the *Times of India*, with the headline "Well-Known Intellectual Now a Buddhist Nun."

> Mrs. Freda Bedi, once a writer, professor, and politician is now a Buddhist bikshuni, running an order of nuns. Dressed in saffron [sic] and with shaved head, Freda Bedi retains her warm, friendly style of conversation. She remains the informal intellectual that she was in Lahore, in pre-Partition days, when thousands often thronged to her meetings to listen to a white Oxford graduate denounce British imperialism. She is the only Buddhist nun of her stature in India.
>
> She rose high in the Mahayana hierarchy through a long process of service. In fact she chose Mahayana mainly because of its stress on service to humanity. Her daily prayer begins with "May I attain enlightenment for the sake of all that live." This life is in accordance with her childhood dreams of prayer

and meditation and her youthful commitment to serve the poor.

Whether intentionally or not, Freda had set the ball rolling for another revolution—a feminist revolution within Tibetan Buddhism. Two years later, Diane Perry, now known globally as Tenzin Palmo, the English girl from the East End of London who had worked for Freda at the Young Lamas Home School in Dalhousie and who had become a nun at the age of twenty-one, followed Freda to Hong Kong and became the second bikshuni. It was the beginning of a great groundswell to reinstate the higher ordination for all Tibetan nuns, and give them equal opportunities.

Today the fight that Freda started still goes on. While the Dalai Lama publicly backs equal spiritual opportunities for women, the male-dominated, conservative Tibetan monastic establishment resists. In the meantime many devoted nuns have found their way to Hong Kong or Taiwan to be fully ordained.

On the news of Freda's second ordination, BPL moved to Milan, on the invitation of an Italian woman, Antonia Chiappini, many years his junior, who had been a patient of his "vibrational healing" in Delhi. He started the Centro Eta Del Acquaria (The Center for the Age of Aquarius), and over time attracted a large, elite clientele. He and Freda kept in frequent, fond touch by mail, and BPL only married Antonia after Freda had died.

By the beginning of 1972, Freda's health was starting to fail. She had only five years left to live, but in that time she would perform arguably her greatest work yet—bringing Buddhism to the West.

The dates listed here are approximate.

1970. The photograph that still reverently holds a place on the altar of the nunnery Freda founded. The signature reads: "With blessings, Gelongma Mummy." (Courtesy Karma Drubgyu Thargay Ling Nunnery.)

1972. The historical meeting of the sixteenth Karmapa and Muktananda, arranged by Freda and Didi Contractor. The reunion of Buddhism and Hinduism after centuries of Buddhism being absent from its homeland.

1975. Freda accompanies the sixteenth Karmapa on his first ever tour of the United States and Europe. Here, they are pictured at the Grand Canyon in Arizona. (Bedi family archives.)

1976. Freda as a teacher on her tour of the United States and Europe. (Bedi family archives.)

2010. Freda's nuns today grouped under the bodhi tree that she had planted as a sapling at Karma Drubgyu Thargay Ling Nunnery. Kabir is in the middle. (Courtesy Parveen Dusanj Bedi.)

1977. The Bedi children all grown up. Left to right: Ranga, Guli, Kabir. (Bedi family archives.)

1976. The elderly Freda and BPL, standing side by side, both as spiritual teachers. (Bedi family archives.)

15

Spreading the Word

SINGLE-HANDEDLY FREDA had already set the scene for Buddhism to make the historic leap from East to West when she had the foresight to establish the Young Lamas Home School. In 1972, the year of her full ordination as a bikshuni nun, she took another momentous step in that direction by personally agreeing to take the Buddha's message to South Africa, the first of several overseas "missions" she undertook. Her journey there was significant not least because it revealed the full extent of the spiritual authority invested in her by the Karmapa, as well as the scope of the knowledge and personal realizations that she had attained in her relatively new religious path.

The invitation had come from Rosemary Vosse, a theosophist descended from Italian nobility, who had met Freda in India. She had literally begged Freda, now known as Sister Palmo, to come to South Africa, which was being brutally ripped apart by the bloody internal war of apartheid, as blacks fought for equal rights and the end to racial segregation. Nelson Mandela, leader of the African National Congress (ANC), the group that led this fight, was serving a life sentence on Robben Island, a measure intended by the government to cut off the hope he had inspired in his followers. Everywhere, protestors were being beaten and jailed, and a general reign of terror, instigated by the police, hung like a dirty pall over the land.

It was an invitation Freda could not resist. Any notion of racial inequality and suppression of freedom was an immediate clarion call to her. In fact it was in Johannesburg that her hero, Mahatma Gandhi, had formulated his philosophy of peaceful civil resistance, triggered when he was ordered to move from a first-class carriage to a third-class carriage because he was "colored," despite the fact that he was working as a lawyer there and had a valid ticket. The result was Satyagraha, his Doctrine of Truth, which he propagated there for twenty years and which Freda espoused when she became a Satyagrahi.

Her tour was to encompass Johannesburg, Cape Town, Durban, and Port Elizabeth. It started on an auspicious note. Stepping off the airplane and into the terminal, she saw a delicate pink, green, and yellow butterfly still alive in a wastepaper basket. She gently picked it up and put it in a flowerbed. Freda viewed it as a sign. "It had a significance I can't put into words, but something extremely beautiful happened as I entered Africa," she wrote to her family.

She addressed audiences, large and small, who had come as a result of publicity generated by her Tibetan Friendship Group. She was warmly welcomed, and the press was polite. She spoke from university podiums and temple high seats, telling people about her experience of Gandhi and her own time as the first Englishwoman to offer Satyagraha. And then, when the audience was warmed up, she moved on to even more unconventional themes—reincarnation and the Tibetan tulku system—showing them slides of the young rinpoches she had taught and of her own teacher, the Sixteenth Karmapa.

"I tried to convey to them something of the wonder of the Tibetan masters, the Dalai Lama, and in particular my own guru," she said. The university students were especially rapt, she reported.

Her talks to the Indian community living there and to the small group of Buddhist sympathizers were more profound, and they allowed Freda to share the depth of her knowledge. She gave discourses on both major and minor points of Buddhist philosophy.

"I was able to give a talk on the realizations of Milarepa (Tibet's beloved poet-saint). I endeavored to bring out his philosophical approach as well as his beautiful teachings, which were based on the Vajrayana lyrics, which I translated. This talk was taped, as were many others," she stated.

More impressively, Freda also revealed that she conferred initiations. This was nothing short of extraordinary. Only the most qualified lamas gave initiations, ceremonies that bestowed on the recipient the power, knowledge, and blessings of the particular buddha invoked. It was exceptional for a newcomer to Buddhism to be conducting this rite, and it was unheard of for a Western woman to do so. This was proof that the Karmapa held her in high spiritual regard.

"On Easter Sunday I was able to give the Forest Dolma (Tara) initiation, which His Holiness Karmapa had allowed me to confer. It was in a perfect setting, in a forest glade with pine needles all around, and the shrine at the foot of a tress," enthused the nature-loving Freda. She continued to give the Tara initiation throughout her tour. And then she ventured into the highly esoteric and advanced reaches of Tibetan Buddhism—the Vajrayana or Diamond Path—by conferring the initiation of the buddha of purification, Vajrasattva.

"I explained how to meditate on Vajrasattva, and say his hundred-syllable mantra," she explained. "It was a most interesting experience to be giving these teachings, and I do think that if the group carries on with the practice, there will be a quick and wonderful development, because the Vajrayana path is more rapid than the Mahayana path. But all the time I am weaving in the Mahayana. The Vajrayana is the meditation side, the Mahayana, the philosophy," she went on, indicating the highly arcane and intricate system of Tibetan Buddhism that Thomas Merton, the Jesuit, described as the most complex religion on earth. "It is complex and detailed because it is profound," said Freda.

Following her plan to sow permanent seeds of Buddhism in South Africa, Freda established small centers, often in people's homes, where people could gather to meditate, say prayers together, and study the Buddha's teachings. She fervently hoped the centers would grow.

Although she fell instantly in love with the natural beauty of Cape Town, she was utterly dismayed by the absence of black faces in the suburbs she was visiting. This was apartheid at work.

"I was surprised to see so few Africans about—they are living in outside areas. You do see them in shops and streets, but Cape Town has such a Western appearance. I was not prepared for that. I rather thought it would be like India, where there would be big houses and a lot of simple houses around. Instead it is like being in Switzerland or Holland—there are hardly any black or brown faces visible."

Much to her delight, she did manage to introduce one African into Buddhism, when she gave the Refuge ceremony to a gathering at a home belonging to Bruce Ginsberg (later famous for introducing rooibos tea to the rest of the world).

"She was a housemaid and was extremely delighted to get it. It gave me some personal satisfaction too," Freda admitted. "Actually Buddhism is not a conversion religion—and I cannot seek people out to give the teachings to, as much as I want to. We have to wait until people come voluntarily. That is how it should be," she added.

Despite being forbidden to proselytize, Freda was nevertheless openly thrilled when she was called upon to officiate at the funeral of a Chinese seaman who had been murdered in Port Elizabeth. Her fame as the only ordained Buddhist in South Africa had spread, much to the gratification of the sailor's Buddhist family. Freda saw it as yet another sign that her religion would take root in South African soil. Officiating at the cremation ceremony, Freda once again revealed her spiritual credentials when she performed the esoteric rite of *powa*—the transference of consciousness—a highly accomplished process whereby a "master" steers the departing mind, or soul, through the death process into a favorable future existence.

"I was able to use the Amitabha Puja for the first time in English," she elaborated, referring to the ritual of the Buddha of Infinite Light, much beloved of the Chinese. "I also made use of the teachings of powa, which the Venerable Ayang Tulku [an eminent reincarnate lama recognized as a living expert in afterlife rituals] gave me in Mysore. It was miraculous I had it with me. By 'chance' I also had a special mandala from Rumtek to be used at the time of somebody's passing. Whatever I could do, I did, praying for the liberation of his mind into the luminous states of consciousness, which is the buddha-field. I also drafted a telegram to H. H. Karmapa in Sikkim to do special ceremonies for the seaman.

"Many people there had never seen Buddhist rites before, and they were deeply moved. We felt it was extraordinary that the first Buddhist nun to reach South Africa was able to be in Port Elizabeth on the very day that the seaman needed help," she added.

She continued on her whistle-stop tour, founding centers, giving talks, and meeting would-be Buddhists. She was particularly happy when she came across the Indian community, who took her into their homes. "'They helped stanch my homesickness at being severed from the motherland. It's a group of some thirty-five Indian families, who have kept the flag of Dharma flying here. I gave them the initiation of Jetsun Dolma in her form as the Perfection of Wisdom," she said, indicating the zenith of the wisdom path, "Emptiness," which is represented by the female form, out of which all things are made manifest.

Sheila Fugard, who met Freda in South Africa, was won over. She was the wife of the internationally renowned playwright Athol Fugard, as well as a poet and author in her own right, and was in a distressed state due to the constant harassment she and her husband were receiving from the police. Athol was courageously defying apartheid by writing and staging political plays, such as *Blood Knot* for a group of multiracial actors, and they were under perpetual surveillance as a result, with their house regularly being ransacked. It was a situation Freda understood only too well from her own experience of being harassed and pursued during her defiant fight for Indian independence. To Sheila, Freda, or Sister Palmo as she called her, was a veritable lifeline. Her devotion became absolute, as depicted in the book she wrote about her, *Lady of Realisation*.

"We were going through a very tough time. I was under enormous stress and was just coming out of a nervous breakdown. We had no money and yet were still trying to create a new theater for all races, but the government was forbidding us to go into the townships, where the blacks lived," said Sheila, now living in California with her daughter.

There was also a lesser-known, religious component to apartheid. "The Dutch Reformed Church felt that blacks should have separate churches, and were fighting with the Catholics who wanted to open the churches to blacks. Sister Palmo was invited in order hopefully to help sow seeds of harmony through establishing Buddhism, and teaching meditation," she explained before continuing with her own story:

"I knew nothing about Buddhism apart from reading Evans-Wentz (an early translator of Tibetan texts, including *The Tibetan Book of the Dead*). I was desperately seeking some means of achieving inner stillness, and had visited several teachers, including Sufis and Hindu swamis. They had offered advice and explanations as regards the nature of the mind, meditation, and the problems of living, but none really helped. The knots of personality remained unsolved.

"I went to a lecture Sister Palmo was giving in a private house. As I walked in, I was met by a sight I had never seen before—a middle-aged Englishwoman sitting in the lotus position, wearing maroon robes with a shaved head. There was no doubt she was beautiful, with a firm bone structure and skin, which, although aging, had a unique softness. She emanated a tranquility, an aura of profound compassion, and what could only be described as an elevated energy. There was an aspect of the yogi about her that fascinated me, and yet at the same time she was undisputedly the Western intellectual.

"What she said was interesting enough to draw me back to listen to her again. By the third time, I thought, 'Forget everything else, this is it.' I signed up for an initiation and a retreat. I was so glad I did. And I also took Refuge with her. The experience was unforgettably powerful," she reminisced.

Freda also had secular words of wisdom to offer regarding apartheid, telling her audience that the intellectuals invariably suffered in any repressive regime. "Such situations toughen the moral fiber," Freda told them. "Tenacity is at the root of *sila*, or morality, the very bedrock of Buddhism. And nonviolence is only understood through experience."

It was in the personal arena, however, where Freda provided the most comfort to Sheila Fugard.

On hearing about her breakdown and the traumas she was going through Freda said, "Well, you know, what you are talking about is suffering. That was the Buddha's main message, it was the foundation of what he taught. But if you think of the mind like a lake, while the surface may be ruffled and agitated by waves, in the depths it is very calm and still.

"Mind is radiantly pure. Emptiness, the primordial ground, underlies both samsara (the Wheel of Suffering) and nirvana. The world of meditation is of extraordinary beauty. In mastering concentration all concepts and confusion fall away. All is attainable by the pupil, but initiations by the guru, proper instruction, and firm endeavor are necessary.'

The effect of Freda's words was immediate and electric. "With those words Sister Palmo changed my life," said Sheila. "She made me realize that that was how it was. Suffering is there, clear and simple, and yet there is a way out. I understood that there was a deep reservoir of peace available to me beneath the fear and anxiety. From that moment I turned a corner and came out of my depression. Things slowly began to improve. She was an excellent teacher and had the clearest view of the Path of any Tibetan master I later met. She had a unique ability to cut through. She was also extremely articulate, the result of her education and talent as a writer and teacher."

As with all truly effective teachers, however, it was the unspoken qualities that Freda embodied that made an equally powerful impression on Sheila. Qualities including compassion, empathy, kindness, and a sense of humor, gained from a deep understanding of the Path, and literally embodied.

"Aside from her words it was her manner itself that was healing. She reached me at a human level. Sister Palmo became a role model, not just for me but for many women, because of all that she had been through and because she was powerful. Her life was vast. She'd been a conservative Englishwoman, an intellectual who had fitted in with a Sikh family, who had got involved in Indian politics, who knew Indira Gandhi and who had had a family before her inner path took over. She was extraordinary. I was her student, and was devoted as well as highly respectful of her," said Sheila.

When she flew out of South Africa, Freda left behind the Karma Rigdol centers she had established in Cape Town, Johannesburg, and Port Elizabeth, all under the auspices of H. H. Karmapa, and a small but enthusiastic group of people committed to following the Buddhist path. Many, like Sheila Fugard, had taken Refuge with Freda, and had been given Tibetan names. Others, like Andre de Wet, became ordained taking a monk's name—in his case, Karma Samten.

She left her new converts with texts of prayers and rituals in English that she had translated herself from the Tibetan. This in itself was an innovative step forward in the bringing of Buddhism to the West, as for many years after the Tibetan diaspora newly engaged Buddhists were obliged to read prayers and chants in the original, without knowing what they were reading and saying.

Over the ensuing years she remained in constant contact with them through her usual stream of letters, guiding their newly formed centers in precise detail: suggesting candidates for the roles of president, secretary, or treasurer according to each person's personality and ability, which she had witnessed and assessed. As with her own children, she was liberal with advice: "Youth are the breath of any new movement, but we need the older students to give stability, those who have seen something of the sorrows of the world. They have more staying power and more understanding of continuity, which is important." Multitasking, also as usual, she set up journals, sent articles, and tried tirelessly (in vain) to get visas for eminent lamas such as Ayang Rinpoche to visit the centers to inspire them anew. When that did not work, she encouraged her students to come to India so that they could experience for themselves what it was like to be in the presence of the freshly emerged meditation masters from Tibet, and get their blessing that way.

Personally on several occasions Freda tried to return to South Africa herself, battling for months to get another visa, but to no avail. The authorities would not let her in. Unbeknownst to her, time was running out. And she still had much to do and bigger territories to conquer.

16

Forging the Bridge

RETURNING TO RUMTEK after her South African tour, Freda resumed her duties as secretary and adviser on worldly affairs to the Sixteenth Karmapa, as well as her translation work and vast correspondence, which she actively enjoyed, finding letter writing relaxing. Her faithful attendant, the nun Pema Zangmo, constantly by her side, actually witnessed the seminal moment when Freda persuaded the Karmapa to journey to the West to introduce the Buddha's teachings to the United States and Europe.

"I heard Mummy-la beg His Holiness Karmapa, 'Please, please go to the USA and Europe. There is no Dharma there, but the West is now truly ready. The young people especially are crying out for the wisdom of the Buddha. In the future, Buddhism will grow in the West—and there will be many centers. Go, go and see with your own eyes,'" she said from her own nunnery.

The Karmapa had been repeatedly asked to visit North America and Europe, but had always declined, probably on the same grounds that deterred most high-ranking lamas—the belief that Westerners were simply too spiritually unevolved to appreciate, let alone grasp, the sophisticated and profound doctrines contained within Tibetan Buddhism. They were right. Until then Buddhism was generally so unknown beyond the East that it was commonly regarded as nothing more than idol worship. Few realized that the core of Buddhism was an advanced understanding of the human mind from the grossest to the subtlest levels of consciousness. The vastness of mind, they maintained, equaled the limitless boundaries of the universe, accessed only through the exploration of inner space, called meditation.

In Rumtek the Karmapa listened to Freda's heartfelt plea. "Fetch the calendar," he said. Leafing through it, he stopped on a page. "September fifteenth," he announced. The year was 1974. What seemed like a random date, whimsically chosen was, according to Freda, in fact the display of a vast mind scanning the universe to settle on the most auspicious intersection of time and space to help usher in the historic event of Tibetan Buddhism's entrance to the West. The decision may have been the Karmapa's, but the catalyst was indisputably Freda, who had the extraordinary foresight to see what lay in store.

The time was definitely ripe. By the early 1970s other lamas had also heard the call. In 1974, Lama Thubten Yeshe and his heart disciple, Lama Zopa Rinpoche, from the Gelugpa School, taught their first meditation course to a group of Australians, at Diamond Valley, Queensland. Courses in England, America, and Europe followed, beginning with small front-room gatherings and rapidly mushrooming into a vast international organization, the Foundation for the Preservation of the Mahayana Tradition (FPMT), comprising not only centers of learning but social and publishing enterprises as well. From the Kagyu School came Kalu Rinpoche, who set up centers in the United States and Europe. H. H. Sixteenth Karmapa, however, bearing a longer lineage than that of the Dalai Lama, was the senior-most lama to set foot on Western soil. It was an enormous coup on Freda's part.

Other forms of Buddhism were also appearing at this time. A small but powerfully enthusiastic group of young Jewish Americans —Jack Kornfield, Sharon Salzberg, and Joseph Goldstein—were transporting Therevada Buddhism in the form of Vipassana, or Insight Meditation, which they had learned in Burma and Thailand. The result was Spirit Rock, in California, and the Insight Meditation Center in Massachusetts, both of which now see thousands of people passing through their doors yearly. Zen Buddhism was also becoming firmly rooted. The Japanese master Shunryu Suzuki Roshi had established the San Francisco Zen Center as early as 1959, popularizing his message through renowned works such as *Zen Mind Beginner's Mind.*

Why the flame of Buddhism should leap from East to West at this particular moment in time is a mystery. Throughout its long history, Buddhism, like a candle flame, had leaped from country to country when the time was right, taking on the color and shape of the culture in which it landed. Consequently, while the core of the Buddha's doctrine, the Four Noble Truths, remained constant, the faces of Japanese, Chinese, Sri Lankan, Thai, Vietnamese, Burmese, Cambodian, Laotian, and Tibetan Buddhism looked very different. Such was the malleability of the Buddha's message, which eschewed dogma and blind faith. "Treat my teachings like gold. Test them and shape them into an ornament to suit each particular wearer," he said. Now Western Buddhism was about to be born, mingling successfully with the discoveries in science, especially quantum physics, neuroscience, and psychotherapy. As such, it was peculiarly "modern," even though it was historically older than both Christianity and Islam.

Whatever the cause of Buddhism's appearance in the West, the timing was perfect. By the early 1970s the youthquake started in the 1960s of free love, miniskirts, drugs, and rock and roll was in full swing. The postwar baby boomers had grown up and were overthrowing the old conservative order, looking for love, peace, and an alternative to their materialistic society. They headed East to find spirituality and gurus, and a new way of living. At the same time the great flood of Tibetan refugees was converging on India. The two rivers met. Like Freda, the young, open, well-educated Westerners were bowled over by the sheer quality of the powerfully charismatic, scholarly lamas who were living out the teachings of wisdom and compassion.

With her plan for the Karmapa's first visit approved, Freda immediately wrote to Chögyam Trungpa, who was already in America, to tell him the good news and ask him to help make arrangements for the tour.

In the end Freda was to make two journeys, in 1974 and 1975–76, traveling through California, Vermont, New York, Colorado, Montreal, Toronto, and then Scotland, Denmark, Norway, Sweden, Germany, Holland, France, and Italy. At times she went ahead, rousing the people to the Karmapa's coming with speeches as eloquent and persuasive as any she delivered to the masses in the bygone days of Indian independence.

"It is really wonderful how His Holiness Karmapa and other great lamas with their actions remind you of the Buddha. You can see the Buddha walking—the gestures of their bearing, their dignity. I'm saying this from my own heart, not just mouthing what is said in the texts. I am sure when His Holiness comes, you will have an amazing experience of seeing a buddha, an Awakened One, walking before you. He will explain the Dharma in a peaceful voice, and tell us how to meditate. All men [sic] who have faith can see it. If you have no faith, you can't see it," she said to a gathering in New York.

"When we see it, a great longing arises in us, to be always near him, to listen to him, to understand," she continued. "Through this great wish our hearts are inspired and we attain the lands of our heart's desire. When we see the Buddha acting in this way without premeditation, we realize he acts not just for any one person or with any bias but for the sake of all, the greater good of all. When your mind sees things in this way, the well-being of all is accomplished, stage by stage.

"Going back to my own experience with His Holiness Karmapa, if he is coming at this time to the United States, it must be that certain people and pupils, young and old, are in their hearts needing his arrival, otherwise he would not come. The lama never comes unless there is a great tide that draws him, because his activity is truly spontaneous and unceasing," she said.

At other times she traveled with the Karmapa, explaining Western culture to him and doing what she did better than anyone else—organizing timetables, meetings, and spiritual engagements, including the highly esoteric Black Crown ceremony, which he performed on a number of occasions to small groups of ten to fifteen people. The recipients may not have realized it, but it was an exceptionally powerful introduction to Tibetan Buddhism, one that the Karmapa hoped would leave a strong, lasting impression. Only the Karmapa could confer it.

It was said that the original Black Crown was woven from the hair of *dakinis*, high female spiritual beings who helped genuine practitioners on their path to awakening. The Crown hovered over the head of each successive Karmapa, granting instant enlightenment to those whose vision was pure enough to see it. A visible replica was made in the fifth century, which the Karmapa was now carrying to the United States and Europe to show to Westerners for the first time in history. During the ritual he would hold it high, trusting that he was making a direct, intuitive connection to his new acolytes, rendering them open to receive the Buddha's blessings.

Freda conceded that traveling with and looking after the Karmapa was an exhausting and sometimes eccentric business. An avid animal lover, His Holiness had chosen to bring along on his grand tour not just the precious Black Crown but a veritable menagerie. It was not easy, as Freda explained in a letter to her family:

"The Karmapa travels with hundreds of birds. We have eight huge birdcages, three dogs, including a white Pekingese puppy. His Holiness's idea of relaxing is to go into a local bird store. He can't leave without buying something—first it was finches and canaries, now he's into parakeets. He's planning to take them around Europe with him, which in winter will be no mean thing. I'm going to have to find ways of heating and feeding them."

A crowd of dignitaries and celebrities made their way to the Karmapa's door, including the Beat poets Allen Ginsberg, Lawrence Ferlinghetti, and Michael McClure. Ginsberg had met the Karmapa previously in Rumtek and was already a devotee. Now, in America, he wanted to know if taking LSD was a valid gateway into the spiritual path. The Karmapa replied that meditation was the only valid way of reaching authentic higher states of consciousness and that taking drugs was merely ersatz ecstasy. Ginsberg's response is not known.

During her travels Freda also met a woman who was to become one of the most influential and respected teachers of our time, Pema Chödrön, disciple of Chögyam Trungpa and abbess of Gampo Abbey, in Nova Scotia, the first Tibetan monastery in America.

Born Deirdre Blomfield-Brown in New York in 1936, she had been twice married and twice divorced before she met Freda. She was seriously considering taking robes, but as a mother with children she was conflicted. Pema Chödrön acknowledges that Freda played a leading role in helping her make up her mind.

"She encouraged me greatly. The fact that she was a mother herself before becoming a nun served as an example that I, with two teenage children, could also take robes. She was actually there as a mentor at my novice ordination with His Holiness Sixteenth Karmapa. And she continued to encourage and support me in my monastic life when I met her again in California a year later," Pema Chödrön said.

Her other memories reveal a surprisingly frank and intimate aspect of Freda's personality. "I remember she told me that after I was ordained, I should not get confused if I felt sexual energy. She said that due to my openness now as a nun I might be quite attractive to men. She advised me just to experience the sexual energy as similar to being a fresh young flower with lots of juice and to let the energy open me up to the world. As she put it, 'Feel the energy but keep your vows faithfully.'

"Of course, it was highly unusual to see a Western Buddhist nun at that time. She was an inspiring woman, given her strength of character and the esteem in which His Holiness Karmapa, and the other monks, held her. Sister Palmo was very strong and daring, willing to go where others had not, but also on the surface a warm but proper British lady."

Chögyam Trungpa Rinpoche, who had arrived in the United States four years previously, was already taking America by storm with his brilliant teachings wrapped in very unconventional packaging. Greeting Freda in a suit and tie, Trungpa was a very different person from the young man who had lived with her and her family in Delhi. As an opening gesture he introduced her to his nine year-old son, Ösel, conceived by a Tibetan nun on the roof of her very own Young Lamas Home School in Dalhousie. Freda had had no idea. He also walked with a limp, the result of a car accident in 1969 while he was still abbot of Samye Ling in Scotland. He was fond of alcohol, often appearing drunk in public, and was openly having affairs with some of his students, all with the knowledge of his English wife, Diane Pybus, whom he had married when she was sixteen.

In spite of his somewhat scandalous behavior, Freda's intuition that Trungpa had special gifts for transmitting Buddhism to the West was being borne out. By leaving his old friend Akong Rinpoche in Scotland and moving to America he rightly believed that he would be able to express the Buddha's teachings in a totally fresh way, unfettered by the rigid traditionalism of Tibetan monastic culture. Now his love and command of English, including poetry, honed at Oxford, was evident in his teachings and books, which revealed not only his grasp of the language but his understanding of the Western mentality. By the time Freda and the Karmapa arrived, Trungpa had already captured the Americans' imagination with his best-selling book *Cutting Through Spiritual Materialism* and his brilliant series of lectures titled "Crazy Wisdom," which he declared was "the heart blood of his lineage" and which he delivered to an audience of some fifteen hundred people.

His flair and imagination was also evident in the way he linked the Buddha's message and methodology to calligraphy, haiku, dressage, ikebana, theater, cinema, and psychology. His brilliance and success were called into question by his behavior, however.

Freda's impressions of her dazzling, unorthodox adopted son in America are recorded in her letters to her husband. As always, she was not keen to judge, but that did not stop her from reprimanding him like a recalcitrant child who needed to be put right.

"Trungpa in his suit and tie is different from our tulku floating about in robes, but in essence the same. A rather stronger aspect, both smiling and semiwrathful. He is doing a vast and highly significant type of mind training. It's Dharma work, putting things right at the grass roots. His methods are both tough and sometimes cutting, perhaps a shade too much so—and perhaps that was why my visit and the Mother touch was needed at that point," she wrote to BPL.

To Trungpa's students, however, she adopted a far more diplomatic, conciliatory tone: "Trungpa teaches in a certain way. He's got a very wrathful way of bringing you to your own understanding," she told students at Trungpa's center Tail of the Tiger (Karmê Chöling) in Vermont. "The quality of the lama is a merciful heart, like the heart of Chenrezig, but sometimes the merciful heart is disguised in an angry form. He can really expose you to many things in yourself that you are unconscious of. That's the wind removing the clouds. As Rinpoche says, 'Idiot compassion is not the point.' There is a greater compassion, which can manifest in many ways," she said.

Freda was not only serving the Karmapa during her overseas trips, however; she was also building up her own spiritual base for the future. She actually opened a small center, Tangye Karma Ling, in San Mateo, California, with the help of a devoted student, Barbara Petty, and confided that she hoped to go there regularly in the future to teach. Sadly the center later burned down, causing much of Freda's written work to be lost.

"The center belongs to the Karmapa, and I have come in as teacher, the first member of the sangha. I had to make a decision at this stage of my life. I really shouldn't be doing all this touring. California is perfect, it is so open and the climate is good, unlike England, where I could have taught," she said in a radio interview.

Freda was also busy giving lectures, radio interviews, and a large number of initiations in her own right, as she had in South Africa.

A letter to BPL, now living in Italy, excitedly reveals her American agenda and the spiritual openness she found there. "I taught a great deal on mantra, the Divine Mother, and the deeper philosophy of the naturally pure mind (*Gyud Lama, or Mahayana Uttaratantra Shastra*). I also created the climate for the coming of Chenrezig (the Buddha of Compassion) in his earthly form, His Holiness Karmapa. There is such a vital new life movement in the States that the old religions in their Christian form have no meaning—which many Church people themselves recognize. There is a great deal of interreligious fellowship among the discerning. Looking at it from a Buddhist point of view, it is fertile for the perennially new Dharma, grounded in reality and not too tied to Tibetan, Japanese, or any national idiom."

Illustrating her point about the readiness of America to accept

Buddhism, she gave a White Tara initiation (the female Buddha of Compassion in Action) in New York, which was simultaneously broadcast on local radio. It was an unprecedented break with tradition and a real entry of Buddhism into modern Western life.

Through the airwaves Freda's voice rang out: "Visualize enlightenment in the form of the Holy Mother, in order to receive all the blessings," she said. "The mind is a tremendous thing. If we can remove the veils, the obscurations, we can see the mirror-like quality of its pure state," she continued. "The Divine Mother helps us calm our minds and brings us the blessing of transcendental knowledge. She also increases life and gives us more energy."

She went on to explain further the esoteric meaning behind Tara: "Tara comes in twenty-one basic forms, whose primary functions are to remove all fears. There is a multiplicity of forms, but in fact there is just one. All is Buddha, all is Divine Mother. It's like fragmentation of light into prismatic colors."

In a moving conclusion to the broadcast Freda ended the initiation with a demonstration of her own motherly concern for all living beings: "I send blessings of the Buddha to every home and garden. There are many lonely people who listen to the radio. I send special prayers to them, and to the old and the sick, and to those who live in the radio more than more fortunate people do. I pray that by the blessings of the Buddha, Dharma (teachings), and Sangha they may cross the ocean of suffering and that all others may cross it too."

If anyone was privately wondering on what authority Freda was dispensing such blessings and initiations, she addressed the issue herself, with due modesty:

"Every teacher before giving an empowerment must speak of their authority and competence to do so. I have heard the Dalai Lama speak very humbly of his own attainment before conferring a great initiation he was about to give in India. With this in mind it is hard for me to present my own accomplishments. Simply believe I have the authority and the ability to bestow this initiation."

Regardless of whether her audience simply believed her authority or not, Freda ventured farther into the realm of Vajrayana, known as the Diamond Vehicle, the Tantric Buddhism exclusive to Tibet.

On several occasions she donned the mantle of the Tantric master, conferring these advanced initiations into the most esoteric deities of the Buddhist pantheon, reading the texts first in Tibetan and then in the English translation. It was further evidence of her spiritual status and personal attainment. Modern American audiences may not have been aware how highly irregular it was for a nun to be performing such rituals in public, high Tantric initiations being strictly the domain of the lamas. In truth what Freda was doing was extraordinary.

She taught the highly secret *Six Yogas of Naropa*, a system of yogic exercises designed to enhance enlightenment. And, ever keen to promote the female face of the Buddha, she conferred the initiation of Vajrayogini, one of the most powerful female Tantric deities, as well as that of Niguma, an eleventh-century yogini famed for founding a lineage and for her supernatural powers.

Following one Tara initiation she gave in America, Freda revealed that the Karmapa had told her she was named after an eighth-century nun in India, a Sister Palmo, who was associated with Tara and who was bestowed with exceptional caring skills. Freda had translated a text about this original Sister Palmo, which she now made available. One of the attendees read it out as a tribute to Freda:

"One should imagine the form of a woman with yellow robe who lived in a hermitage, following the path of the yogi, dwelling in a forest, living a life of seclusion and meditation. Gelongma Palmo showed herself in her outer form as the bikshuni—a fully ordained nun with an ushnisha mound on her head, like the Buddha. In her inner form she manifested as Tara, green in color, removing obstacles and hindrances (to enlightenment). Thinking of Gelongma Palmo in this form, we should recollect the very beautiful initiation of the Green Mother, which we experienced this morning."

The references and allusions were obvious. Freda clearly identified with the eighth-century nun, and she wanted others to see her that way as well.

On her last trip to the United States, exhausted, she managed to find time for a solitary two-week meditation retreat at Mount

Shasta. Eyewitnesses reported that she emerged quite radiant. The retreat coincided with her tenth anniversary as a nun, after which she was regaled with a large party, complete with cake, candles, and musicians. Allen Ginsberg and Lama Karma Thinley were among the guests.

Tired, but determined to complete the tour, she accompanied the Karmapa to Europe. The schedule was as busy as ever. Among the spiritual programs, Freda organized a meeting for the Karmapa with Pope Paul VI, and found time to visit BPL in Italy. In Scotland she went to Samye Ling, to catch up with Akong Rinpoche, and popped in to see her niece, Pauline Watson, the daughter of her late beloved brother, John, who was living nearby with her family.

Pauline remembers the visit well. "The neighbors couldn't believe their eyes, this bald white woman in red robes. All the curtains were twitching. My overriding impression was one of spirituality. It came into the room with her. We sat down in a circle and she led us in saying a mantra. It was quite lovely. There was a calmness about her, and she was extremely kind, especially to the children. She stayed with us for a few days and took us to Samye Ling."

Touching base with her own culture, she listened to carols sung by the sublime King's College Choir in Cambridge, then bought Earl Grey tea, and a Beatrix Potter book for her grandchildren.

Time was running out. Freda was exhausted, overweight, and clearly unwell. A radio recording she made in 1975 reveals her gasping for breath. In San Francisco a doctor diagnosed a heart condition, and those close to her felt a poignancy when she left. Trungpa Rinpoche in particular saw what was coming. On saying farewell to his surrogate mother, mentor and friend, he said, "I shall not see you again, but after the passing of time we shall be united."

By the time Freda and the Karmapa reached Paris, her exhaustion was total. She came down with a heavy bout of flu, which laid her very low. But to her it had all been worth it. "Thousands of people have now seen His Holiness Karmapa and witnessed the Black Crown ceremony, which has extraordinary vibrations and carries a liberating effect on the mind," she said.

As usual she had given it her all—traveling many thousands of miles, dispensing spiritual words in many different cities, towns, and villages across the Western world, and speaking to countless people. "I've been pretty besieged," she admitted, "but it's comforting for people to have someone to speak to in their own language."

When it was over, she limped back to Sikkim and her room high up in the monastery of Rumtek. "I always want to come back to India. It feels like coming home," she said.

17

Last Days

RELIEVED TO BE BACK in "the motherland" and her room in Rumtek Monastery, close to her guru, Freda's health seemed to improve. She visited her children, went into another retreat, studied and translated Tibetan texts, read the histories of the early Karmapas, and took up her pen to answer the huge correspondence from the Tibetan Friendship Group that had piled up in her absence. She was happy.

"The healing vibes from H. H. Karmapa have completed the healing process and I am ninety percent back to normal. Also the care that Ranga and Kabir gave me was wonderful, and Umi is always so sweet. Really it is a blessing of the guru and the Triple Gem that this loving attitude surrounds us in these later years," she wrote fondly to BPL in February 1976.

"The retreat was good and there's a creative way to letter writing. I quite enjoy it. So many need help and advice. I'm concerned with getting the texts out as cheaply and beautifully as possible."

With the faithful Pema Zangmo taking care of her immediate needs, life in Rumtek was satisfying. She had developed a good relationship with many of the locals outside the monastery, who mainly knew her as the mother of the increasingly famous, good-looking film star Kabir Bedi, and her life had settled into a satisfying rhythm:

4:00 a.m., wake up, meditate
7:00 a.m., breakfast (two pieces of toast and a cup of tea)
8:00 a.m., meditation until the Karmapa called her to translate or do other work

11:30 a.m., lunch (two chapatis, vegetables, and occasionally
    a little meat), followed by letter writing, translating texts,
    responding to a multitude of requests for help
3:00 p.m., Thrangu Rinpoche, her abbot, arrived to study and
    translate advanced teachings with her
6:00 p.m., a private Mahakala Puja (an advanced Tantric pro-
    tector practice) with H. H. Karmapa and his heart disci-
    ples, Shamar Rinpoche, Situ Rinpoche, Jamgon Kongtrul
    Rinpoche, and Gyaltsab Rinpoche
8:00 p.m., cup of milk, more meditation
11:00 p.m. bed

At sixty-five years of age Freda was thinking of her old age. With
money donated to her during her world tours, plans were afoot to
build a small cottage, "the Hermitage on the Hill," close to but separated from the bustle of the monastery. The dream of finally having a place of her own where she could live out the remainder of her
days more quietly was hugely enticing.

"The Hermitage is perched on a hill with a really lovely view and
pure air. There is a room for me and Pema Zangmo each, a small
shrine room with bunks and pillows on the floor, a bathroom, and
kitchen. And, if the pennies flow in, there will be a guest room on
the roof with modern conveniences. I'm also designing a six-foot
veranda where I can sit outside during the rain. Of course, I'll have
to pipe in water. And there will be a garden. I'm so looking forward
to gardening again. It's exciting to plan it," she wrote enthusiastically to BPL.

Her dream was more than deserved. Now an elderly woman,
having lived in small one-room monastic cells for years and, before
that, generously sharing her homes, be it The Huts or Delhi flats
with umpteen others—friends and strangers alike—she had earned
a comfortable space of her own.

Rewards were coming from other directions as well. In the
same year, October 1976, her old friend Indira Gandhi, the Indian
prime minister, bestowed on Freda one of forty-six awards given
to "foreign women who had distinguished themselves through

outstanding service to India." In Freda's case, she was recognized for her dedication and achievements in the fields of education and social welfare.

Her trophy was a silver box containing, bizarrely, four volumes of *The Spirit of India*, a biography of Indira Gandhi herself, including her speeches and writings! The inscription read, "To Sister Palmo. In the International Women's Year, the women of India recall your service to India and present this to you as a token of their gratitude."

Publicly, Freda expressed her delight. She immediately informed her old college, St. Hugh's, Oxford, so they could publish her achievement in their newsletter, and wrote again to BPL telling him the good news, revealing in both cases a curious predilection for celebrity that seemed at odds with her robes and vows of renunciation.

"I was frankly surprised that after my fourteen years in the mountains they had remembered me, and touched too. I was also delighted that Freda Bedi had slipped so naturally into Sister Palmo in the Indian 'scene' too, as the anomaly is that Sister Palmo is now fairly well known in the Buddhist world of the West, but she has not yet settled into the consciousness of the Indian plains."

Privately however, Kabir claims his mother was furious.

"She was enraged and hurt that she was regarded as a foreign woman. She had become an Indian national shortly after arriving and thought of herself as Indian. Ever since she'd been a young woman, she had given herself to India. She was planning to refuse the award, but then saw the inevitability of government categories and reasonably conceded that she did have a white skin and was born in England," he said.

Freda spent Christmas 1976 with Ranga, Umi, and her grand-daughters, Ami, seventeen; Sohni, fourteen; and Seher, five, in Calcutta. As she promised when she became a nun, she had never severed her close links with her children, keeping up with their news and well-being through regular correspondence, buying them presents, and when her schedule allowed, meeting them at their respective homes. She was always intimately involved with their personal lives. In her later years, however, it seemed she felt a tug to be physically near them more often.

The moment she arrived in Calcutta, Freda fell ill. Her usual winter cough turned into heavy congestion, affecting her heart, and she spent eleven days in intensive care in a nursing home. She admitted it was a near heart attack.

When she recovered, she declared that she felt better and lighter than ever, and got on with enjoying Christmas. She was disappointed that BPL would not be able to join them. "Italy seems to be his home now—he's very much appreciated there as a guru father figure, and happy. It will be summer before he arrives."

Instead she contented herself with enjoying her granddaughters' talents, charms, and beauty. She hoped Kabir, now a film star, would be able to visit, accompanied by his new girlfriend now that he'd divorced his first wife, the flamboyant classical Indian dancer named Protima. "Kabir is back after a great success on TV in Europe. He has now made his first Italian film, *Black Corsair,*" she wrote proudly to Valerie Grove, from the very active Australian branch of the Tibetan Friendship Group. Guli, now heavily pregnant with her second child, was staying put in Bombay.

"I am looking forward to seeing my daughter again—and shall feel all that much better when baby number two is safely here," she said. The slight note of caution proved to be another of Freda's prescient moments.

Freda enjoyed her last Christmas. She helped decorate the Christmas tree and prepared her famous English trifle, but balked at baking a Christmas cake "because of the appalling price of currants."

New Year 1977 saw Freda making a pilgrimage to Sarnath, where the Buddha taught his first sermon on the Four Noble Truths, and Bodhgaya, in Bihar, where he attained enlightenment. She meditated, lit butter lamps, dispensed sweaters and money to Tibetans and beggars, and then returned to Rumtek.

In early March 1977 one of Freda's inner alarm bells sounded. Guli was in trouble. She immediately caught a plane and rushed to her side.

"Mummy, apparently, was already very worried about the birth, because she told a friend that she *had* to be there," said Guli. "I was induced, eleven days late, and while I was being moved to the delivery ward the labor pains suddenly stopped. The doctor was clearly concerned. Had the drip inducing the labor become unplugged, or had something happened to the baby? When my daughter was born, she wasn't breathing. The doctor gasped and said, 'Oh my God.' The cord was exceptionally long and was wrapped *three times* around her neck. It was a real emergency. The doctor said it was a miracle that Brinda had not only survived but had suffered no brain damage.

"We were just so lucky. When it was over, Mummy took Brinda in her arms and blessed her. Even though Mummy had been absent for much of my life, I knew she always watched over me."

No one suspected, except possibly Freda herself, that it was Freda's life that was in imminent danger. A few days before Brinda's birth, on Pema Zangmo's insistence, she had gone for a thorough medical checkup and been given the all clear.

Happy, she left Guli to get on the Delhi train taking her to her next engagement, the World Buddhist Conference being held at the Vigyan Bhavan Hall, Delhi's premier conference venue. There she settled herself into a luxury suite at the five-star Oberoi Intercontinental Hotel, as a guest of her close friend and devotee Goodie Oberoi, wife of the owner.

March 28, 1977, the day of her death, was an interesting one.

If no one suspected what was coming, Freda herself indicated she knew exactly what was in store. In retrospect Pema Zangmo recalled how Freda had pressed her address book on her, telling her she would need it. She also advised her attendant to bring another nun back with her to Rumtek to help her. Pema Zangmo asked her if she was leaving and if so where she was going. Freda had answered enigmatically, "You don't know. I know." She had then gone through her handbag telling her what was important.

Throughout the day many people spontaneously turned up to visit Freda, many of them from the Tibetan Friendship Group that Freda had founded. She greeted them all warmly and told them about her new project to sponsor Tibetan children in top Indian public schools, especially girls, who had less chance of receiving a good education than boys. During the course of the day she curiously handed over all her signing powers and insisted that Pema

Zangmo get in touch with Binder, BPL's nephew, who had grown up in the Bedi family and was now living in Delhi as a well-known political commentator. Nobody then quite knew why she wanted to make contact with him.

At six p.m. Freda and Pema Zangmo went for a walk, after which Freda settled down to some letter writing. She then took out some of her own childhood photographs and those of her children, taken in Lahore, before Partition. At ten p.m. Freda woke Pema Zangmo to give her instructions about certain gifts and money she wanted her to pass on to specific people. She brought out some yellow fabric as a gift for her faithful attendant to make into a nun's blouse, and told her to practice Dharma faithfully. Freda then dressed herself in her finest robes, telling the curious Pema Zangmo, "I will need them tomorrow." She then put on a tape recording of H. H. Karmapa, which he had sent her from New York, and sat down to meditate.

Pema Zangmo, who had gone back to sleep a few feet away from Freda, was awakened by the sound of "louder breathing." She got up and went over to Freda, who was still sitting bolt upright in the meditation position, and tapped her on the shoulder. Freda did not move, nor open her eyes. Peering closer, Pema Zangmo could detect no sign of outer life at all. In total panic she ran out into the hotel corridor screaming for help. A doctor was quickly summoned, who officially pronounced Freda dead. The cause: cardiac arrest. Pema Zangmo noted that her face wore a soft smile.

Gathering all her wits and Tibetan Buddhist know-how of what to do at the time of death, Pema Zangmo became her fiercest self. "Do not touch her. She is in deep samadhi. Nothing must disturb her," she yelled at everyone present. She knew that although there was no pulse or outer sign of life, internally Freda was far from dead. Her body was warm and not cooling, she was sitting upright, she was in samadhi, the profound meditative state of single-pointed concentration, controlling her most subtle mind toward the final stage of death, the Clear Light and beyond to her next birth. It was the acme of Tibetan Buddhist practice, only accomplished by the most advanced meditators, it was said. Pema Zangmo had no doubts that Freda qualified. The truly adept could stay in this state for days, weeks even, their bodies not decomposing, while they remained in the luminosity of the blissful state of their primordial consciousness, attaining higher and higher degrees of awakening. Those who had taken the Bodhisattva Vow, however, now seized the opportunity to steer their consciousness into a realm or body where they could most benefit others.

Not everyone shared Pema Zangmo's convictions. Kabir, who had seen his mother in Bombay just a few days previously, now rushed to Delhi to see her in death. "I'm always skeptical about religious mythmaking," he said. "When I saw Mummy's body, there was a slight grimace on her face, as though she had been in pain. There wasn't a look of divine bliss." He was in total shock. "When I last saw her, she seemed to be in good health. There was absolutely no reason to think she was going to pass away. Looking back, however, I realized she had given me a hint: 'Life is so fragile. A person can be gone in an instant,' she had said, which struck me as rather odd," said Kabir.

Proving that everyone witnesses events from their own viewpoint, Ranga had a still different impression. "Mummy looked totally calm. There was an extraordinary peace emanating from her. It was bloody hot in that room, and Mummy was in her robes underneath a fan, yet her skin was glowing," he said.

In Milan, BPL, Freda's great earthly love, was utterly devastated by the news. His immediate response was to pour out his grief in a love poem:

The cup of your grace is full, O Lord!
And the cup of my prayers is full, O Lord!
What shall I tell my heart
Till the two cups embrace, O Lord!

Nobody wanted to break the news to Guli, who was still in the hospital with her newborn baby. She heard it from a doctor, who inadvertently blurted out how sorry he was about her mother. The shock was cataclysmic. Guli's milk immediately dried up, and she contracted psychosomatic arthritis, unable to uncurl from a sleeping position for three months.

On March 29 Freda's body was taken to Binder's house in Delhi and laid out on a bed of flowers. The Karmapa was deeply shocked, sent messages of condolences, and strongly advised that her body be taken to Rumtek for cremation. The family, however, decided to cremate Freda in Delhi, on the grounds of the Oberois' farm. It was a decision Ranga was later deeply to regret.

"It was around 104 degrees Fahrenheit in Delhi, and it would have taken three days to arrange to fly Mummy's body to Rumtek. We would have had to embalm her for the flight. Kabir, Binder, and I couldn't do it. Mummy's body would have bloated and we didn't want that," he said. "Mummy was lying on the floor under a fan, and yet after three days there was no iota of change in her at all. On the fourth day we took her to Goodie Oberoi's farm. When the hearse arrived, I helped pick her up and her joints were all soft. There was no rigor mortis. H. H. Karmapa must have known that she would have made the journey to Rumtek without problems."

Nevertheless the funeral on the Delhi farm had its own profound meaning. Near the cremation site, next to a wall of bougainvillea, was a sapling bodhi tree, which had been planted there a month earlier at Freda's suggestion when she had visited the farm with Goodie Oberoi. Goodie had wanted to build a small temple there, and Freda felt it would be auspicious to bless the ground with a replica of the tree under which the Buddha had attained enlightenment.

With fortunate synchronicity Freda's funeral coincided with the opening day of the World Buddhist Conference. It was postponed until two p.m. so that the delegates could pay their respects to the woman who had been the close and beloved disciple of the Karmapa, who had been the first nun to achieve the highest bikshuni ordination, who had tirelessly helped the Tibetan refugees in the greatest hour of their need, and who had been such a powerful diplomat of Buddhism around the world.

According to Kabir, coaches carrying around a hundred robed delegates arrived—Buddhist monks from across the world, including representatives from Russia, who were attending the

Conference for the first time in history. They stood around the pyre chanting and saying prayers. A white cloth was placed on Freda's body, and Ranga lit the pyre. Rather alarmingly, those standing close by saw beads of sweat appear on Freda's face.

"It was an amazing send-off. We knew her life had been devoted to the spiritual, but I had no idea how big she was in the Buddhist world until she died," said Ranga.

Tributes began to pour in acknowledging her many achievements. Her obituary in *The Statesman*, Calcutta, read:

> Mrs. Freda Bedi's was a dedicated life. One of the few British women who made India their home and participated actively in the freedom struggle, she engaged herself, after independence, in social work and religious studies. Deeply influenced by Eastern philosophy, she embraced Buddhism and chose the austere life of a nun so that she could devote all her time to the people and to her faith.
>
> In religion she attained the highest rank of the Mahayana order, and for her social welfare activities she received a special award in the International Women's Year for outstanding contribution to the cause of Indian women. She will be remembered especially for her work among Tibetan refugees.
>
> As her son, Kabir Bedi, says, "Her life was an expression of the spiritual in the most human way—living for the causes she believed in."

More tributes poured in from the ranks of the Tibetan hierarchy. Christmas Humphreys, founder of the Buddhist Society in London, wrote a glowing tribute in their magazine, *The Middle Way*:

> Freda Bedi showed what a Buddhist life should be. For twenty-five years she gave her life with immense and ceaseless energy to all in need of help, whatever their creed or caste or color. She never relaxed or hesitated. If the job was there to do she began it and relied, never in vain, on the needed support to

appear. I saw much of the results of her labor when I was myself in India for the Dalai Lama in 1962, and endorse a remark by Mrs. Carlo Robins: "Freda Bedi is an example to all those adherents to any religion who readily regard their religion as being their life and not merely a department of it." Freda Bedi was a great woman, a great Buddhist and an inspiration to all Buddhists East and West to work unceasingly in the service of mankind.

In his message of condolence to the family, the esteemed master Venerable Ayang Rinpoche, who had taught Freda the mystical rite of the transference of consciousness at the time of death—powa—spoke touchingly and profoundly of what her death meant for many Tibetans, lay and ordained alike:

> The sad news of dear Mummy's death has brought a quivering shock to all of us who knew her in the past and I am sure to those who are still very close to her noble heart. I sat down in deep thought, as our dear Mummy would have done in times of grave situations, and I have decided she has fulfilled her life's goal . . . she was especially like a mother to the cause of Tibetan Buddhists in particular.
>
> The loss of Mummy, therefore, is not only a great deprivation to you and me or the Tibetans alone, but it is a great loss to the whole of mankind. However, at this time, sorrow cannot bring back the loss, and the best that mankind can do is to follow her noble steps. . . . The same event will take place with everyone and it is important to realize this from time to time and devote some of your time to religious practice.

On April 2, Freda's ashes were placed in a beautiful engraved urn and flown to Calcutta, and then taken to Rumtek. Sadly it was the very same flight that had been booked to take Freda to visit Ranga and Umi after attending the World Buddhist Conference. Now Kabir and Pema Zangmo carried the remains back to her monastery, where a forty-nine-day puja (prayer ceremony), commanded by H. H. Karmapa, began—the length of time of the bardo, the intermediate state between death and rebirth.

"Maybe she is in the buddha-fields that she spoke about," mused Ranga in a letter to his father, "but no farther away from any of us than we have always known her to be. She used to say 'Dear, I can't stop you from coming to harm, but my prayers can act like an umbrella in a downpour. You get wet, but you don't get soaked.' And to this extent, whether in life or death, I do not think she will cease to keep this umbrella over us."

But Freda's story may not end there, however.

Two years after her death, in 1979, rumors began to spread that Freda had reincarnated as a Tibetan girl, Jamyang Dolma Lama, the daughter of His Eminence Beru Khyentse Rinpoche, a respected lineage holder enthroned by the Sixteenth Karmapa. Born in Tibet, Beru Khyentse Rinpoche had known Freda Bedi well, and had set up his own center in Bodhgaya.

In 1995, when she was sixteen years old, Jamyang Dolma Lama, now a nun, was officially recognized by her father and other lamas as the reincarnation of Freda Bedi, a.k.a. Sister Kechog Palmo. Since then she has undertaken a nine-year intensive study program at Ngagyur Nyingma Nunnery High Institute, and on February 28, 2015, completed a six-and-a-half-year retreat. Fully qualified to teach, she is destined to take care of her father's nunneries in both India and Tibet and, like Freda, to travel around the world to spread the Buddha's teaching for the benefit of all sentient beings.

For some, like Pema Zangmo, there is no doubt that Freda has reappeared on the earth in a new body. "Mummy-la has come back as a Tibetan girl. I have no doubts. She came to see me at my nunnery and I recognized her immediately and her me. She took my hand, gave me a katag (white ceremonial scarf), and cried. She is very beautiful. When I look at her, I see Mummy-la, not the face but the nature is the same. Just before she died, Mummy-la told me to keep in touch with Beru Khyentse Rinpoche, as the connection was very auspicious," she said portentously, hinting that Freda had already determined her next rebirth.

Freda's children are more noncommittal. Shortly after her mother died, Guli asked the Karmapa if she had reincarnated. "The level your mother reached, she could choose whether to return or not. Knowing your mother, she would probably choose to do so," he said, referring to the adept's ability to choose a specific reincarnation, motivated solely by the altruistic intention to return to this earth purely to help others find the way out of sorrow. This was the bodhisattva's birth, so different from "ordinary" births, thrown willy-nilly by the forces of uncontrolled karma.

It was a suitably diplomatic answer to the delicate, frequently controversial issue of reincarnation, often fraught with political and spiritual power play. The Karmapa's words, however, spoke volumes of the extraordinary life and achievements of the woman called Freda Bedi, the woman who had been a political, social, and spiritual revolutionary, and who had proved conclusively that she cared.

EPILOGUE

WHEN I FIRST HEARD of Freda Bedi on that crisp November morning in 1976, I knew nothing of the woman Lama Yeshe had reverently prostrated to. Now, I have traveled with her via this book through her very extraordinary life and have come to know her through her own words and the generous testimony of others. She has emerged a most vivid, exciting, and complex figure. Starting off on this long odyssey, what I particularly wanted to know was why she earned Lama Yeshe's most unusual homage. And, in particular, did she deserve to be hailed as a female icon?

There is no doubt that Freda Bedi was a heroine. She was extraordinarily brave, wading into battle in the cause of equality and freedom on behalf of the entire Indian nation, the dispossessed, the poor, the sick, the forgotten, the refugees—and women, secular and ordained alike. She seemed to know no fear. She took on secret police, angry mobs, imprisonment, and bears with no thought of her own safety. She was a dauntless champion of women, a passionate feminist, who like the Suffragettes of her own era, believed that deeds, not words, were what mattered.

As Freda began to reveal herself, the woman behind the myriad roles she played took shape. She was full of curious contradictions.

She was an ace administrator, furnished with a steely will, a brilliant mind, a relentless drive, a woman who always knew where she was going. And she was dreamy, given to flights of lyric romanticism and hopeless idealism. Many attested to her imperious manner, dispensing orders and expecting them to be obeyed, and yet she was also universally acknowledged for her warmth and kindness. She was genuinely egalitarian, inviting servants to sit at her table with

diplomats and insisting on herself traveling third class. Yet she min-
gled readily with the highest in the land and was prone to tedious
name-dropping of the great and the good whom she knew. Maybe
she had an eye toward being published. Freda was a high-ranking
Buddhist nun, but she was never shy of fame or self-publicity. Never
forgetting her socialist principles, she eschewed money and own-
ing property. Yet she never balked at accepting invitations to stay
at five-star hotels.

The most intriguing and arguably the most controversial contra-
diction in Freda's makeup rested in her dual roles as Mother. She
gave birth to four children, and yet from the time they were born,
she frequently left them to fulfill her bigger calling as Mother to all
the world. Everyone called her Mummy, for the love and caring she
gave them. Yet one her babies died while she was away campaigning
for the greater good, and she deposited her daughter at age five in
boarding school so that she could follow her Buddhist vocation. She
left Ranga without mother *and* father when she willingly went to
jail, and she rendered the entire family homeless when she gave up
her job to become a nun. Freda's actions flew in the face of accepted
mores that a "good" mother should be prepared to sacrifice *everything* for her children. In society's eyes that selflessness is what gives
a mother special status.

Throughout the book I had to ask myself, "Is it possible for a
woman to be Che Guevara, Mother Teresa, and a physical mother
at the same time? Was Freda really selfish and egotistical for leaving
her children to follow a bigger path? Was I being judgmental, sex-
ist? Fathers who pursue their dreams—climbing Everest, walking
to the South Pole, crossing oceans in small boats, driving racing
cars, or more commonly globe-trotting incessantly in the name of
business are not similarly censured. I concluded that society holds
strong judgments around mothers. Once again it was about gender.

Freda's life choices around mothering also threw into focus
other hot issues, normally not aired. Few dare speak the unmen-
tionable—that not all women are fulfilled by motherhood. Many
mothers cannot wait to get back to work, to escape the demands
and tedium of small children. And newspapers often carry stories

of mothers who have killed their children. Interestingly another great matriarch, Queen Victoria, mother of nine, revealed in her diaries that she hated being pregnant—"It was like being a cow or a dog"—viewed breast-feeding with disgust, and found her children "ugly and repulsive." It was begetting her children with Prince Albert that she enjoyed.

It is not known whether Freda actively wanted children. She was born before the contraceptive pill—the great liberator—was invented, and became pregnant very quickly after her wedding in a day when marriage automatically meant motherhood. From childhood she had been driven by her strong spiritual and social ideals. She loved BPL, but married him as much for his political fervor for Indian independence as for her passion for him. She certainly had never been attracted to domesticity.

During my travels I met one of Freda's friends, an American woman named Didi Contractor, who met Freda in Bombay in 1969. A film-set designer of mud brick houses, and later a leading ecologist, Didi threw an interesting light on many aspects of Freda's personality.

"Because she valued the big picture, I am not sure how strongly she viewed motherhood," said Didi, speaking in one of her own mud huts situated in a small village near Dharamsala. "I think Guli was rather shortchanged. I remember one occasion when she kept trying to tell her mother that she was engaged, but Freda was more interested in talking about Muktananda (my guru) and religion with me. She kept saying, 'Not now, Guli.'

"Freda was unique, a big woman in every sense of the word, imposing and very, very warm. Her voice was strong, confident, and sometimes very dramatic, especially when she was saying prayers! And she could be endearingly pompous and rather sweeping, almost ludicrously so. Because she was so big, it was easy for her to be a big target for negativities. You could see her in either of two ways—comic absorption in her role or total commitment. I loved her, but I wasn't blind to her foibles, as you aren't when you truly love someone," she continued.

"Everything was black-and-white with her—there were no shades of gray. That was exactly what was needed to accomplish what she did. She had a sense of humor but never about herself, and no sense of irony. Mummy always knew best. She would listen to you but not alter her opinion one jot. Whatever she believed in, she did it completely and instantly. She was immensely powerful *because* she believed in herself. At the same time she was extraordinarily naïve—naïve in the way every creative person is. You have to be naïve to complexities in order to embrace things as completely as she did."

In the end I turned to her children, the only people truly qualified to speak on the subject of what kind of a mother she was. Today Ranga, Kabir, and Guli all regard their mother with a great deal of love and even a little reverence. None, however are blind to the difficulties she put them through.

"Looking back I can honestly say I feel truly blessed. As a mother she was really something. For a daughter, she was *fantastic* because she really believed in empowering women," said Guli, the child who saw the least of her mother, and yet the one who grew up to be most like her. Guli inherited Freda's strong independent streak, her brain, and, with her job of teaching disadvantaged children, her commitment to caring for others.

"I was raised to have a voice, make something of my life, and be financially independent. She told me many women were unhappy because they couldn't leave their marriages. She wasn't pleased that I was going to marry an artist, because she knew how hard life could be without money, but she wasn't going to stop me, because she believed in freedom of choice. She had a premonition it wouldn't last—as usual she was right.

"Although I never knew from one month to the next where I was going to be living, I have to admit I never felt neglected or unloved by either of my parents. Mummy was very cuddly.

"Her one great fault was that she saw life through rose-colored glasses. She had a romantic view of life and people. She would only see the good. Kabir and I used to joke about it. If we encountered a mean or unpleasant person, we would turn to each other and say 'They must have inner beauty.' Mummy did not, or would not, see the dark side of people's nature. It could be utterly exasperating. Sometimes she got hurt because of it too."

Guli also found great difficulty in accepting her mother's absolute obeisance to the Karmapa. "I had a raging argument with her
just before she died. 'I can't understand how you, a radical, smart,
decisive, strong woman, an Oxford graduate, who has always been
outspoken and taken responsibility for your actions, now have to
check with your guru before you do anything! Why are you now
handing over everything to him?' She replied, 'Guli, you don't
understand. It's about going into another life—one that is far more
fulfilling.'"

Kabir handled Freda's constant commitment to her work and
her causes very well.

"Of course Mummy was away a lot—which honestly didn't
bother me," he said. "She was driven by her large social conscience.
When she *was* home, she held you and made you feel special and
wanted. The main problem was that she left us homeless when she
took up Buddhism. I worried about Guli, especially as Mummy was
the main breadwinner. There was always the stress of having no
money—my parents just didn't care about it. What *was* important to
them was their principles. They were idealistic to the point of folly.
We children inherited nothing from them except their values."

Ranga, who saw the most of Freda when he was a child, shares
Kabir's feelings.

"Mummy gave me a wonderful life. But because my parents lived
constantly on a knife-edge, I have always felt the need for security.
I wasn't aware of it at the time, but my childhood was very insecure.
Throughout my adulthood I had to be secure in my job, and my
family always comes first. I'm highly protective," he said.

Freda may have been physically absent from her children, but she
attempted to manage their upbringing, down to the smallest details
of their lives, through her letters.

Here's Freda answering Kabir's championing of his sister's need
for pickles at boarding school:

Guli's pickle problem is as follows: Please tell her to be rea-
sonable and not complain. You have given her pickle. I am
sending her a birthday parcel containing jam and pickle. It's

quite absurd anyway that one should not be able to live without jam and pickle rolling in.

And this intimate, though somewhat cryptic letter to Kabir:

Think hard about smoking and the other thing. These all have karmas. It's a law as impersonal as a scientific law that $H_2O =$ water. Smoking affects the mind (leading to attachment) and the body, filling its pure cavities with smoke. There's a tarry deposit from tobacco that causes cancer. Always use filter tips if you must smoke. When I went to college, the girls persuaded me to smoke, and I smoked for three months. Then one day I woke up to the uselessness of it and stopped. I never smoked again.

Kabir didn't heed his mother's advice. Instead he followed in his father's footsteps and is rarely seen without a cigarette.

When letters would not do, Freda became more hands-on. She officiated at Kabir's first marriage to Protima, conducting the ceremony herself. And she'd rush to her children's side when she felt they were in danger.

I concluded that Freda was a woman who had managed to have it all—husband, children, a stellar career, political activism, *and* a religious vocation. Freda did not give up anything. It was no mean feat.

As to Freda being an emanation of Tara, the female Buddha of Compassion in Action, I am in no position to judge. For all her very human shortcomings, she had exceptional compassion, which played out in all the myriad roles she undertook. Like Tara she was indisputably a doer, not content to sit back and bewail the problems of society or merely legislate about them. She jumped right in. Her heart was as wide as the world. Furthermore Freda, like Tara, was highly effective in accomplishing what she set out to do.

Whoever she was, by the end of my journey into her life I understood why Lama Yeshe, in that meditation tent in Kathmandu back in 1976, had prostrated three times before her. I wondered why

Freda's remarkable story had never been told. I concluded that her fate was that of most powerful women in history; she was simply overlooked. It was time to set the record straight. Freda's song deserved to be sung.

ALSO BY VICKI MACKENZIE

*Cave in the Snow: A Western Woman's
Quest for Enlightenment*

*Child of Tibet: The Story of Soname's Flight
to Freedom*, with Soname Yangchen

Reborn in the West: The Reincarnation Masters

Reincarnation: The Boy Lama

Why Buddhism?: Westerners in Search of Wisdom